The Book of Veles
(Vles Knyha)

Translated from the Old Slavonic

by

Victor Kachur

COLUMBUS, OHIO

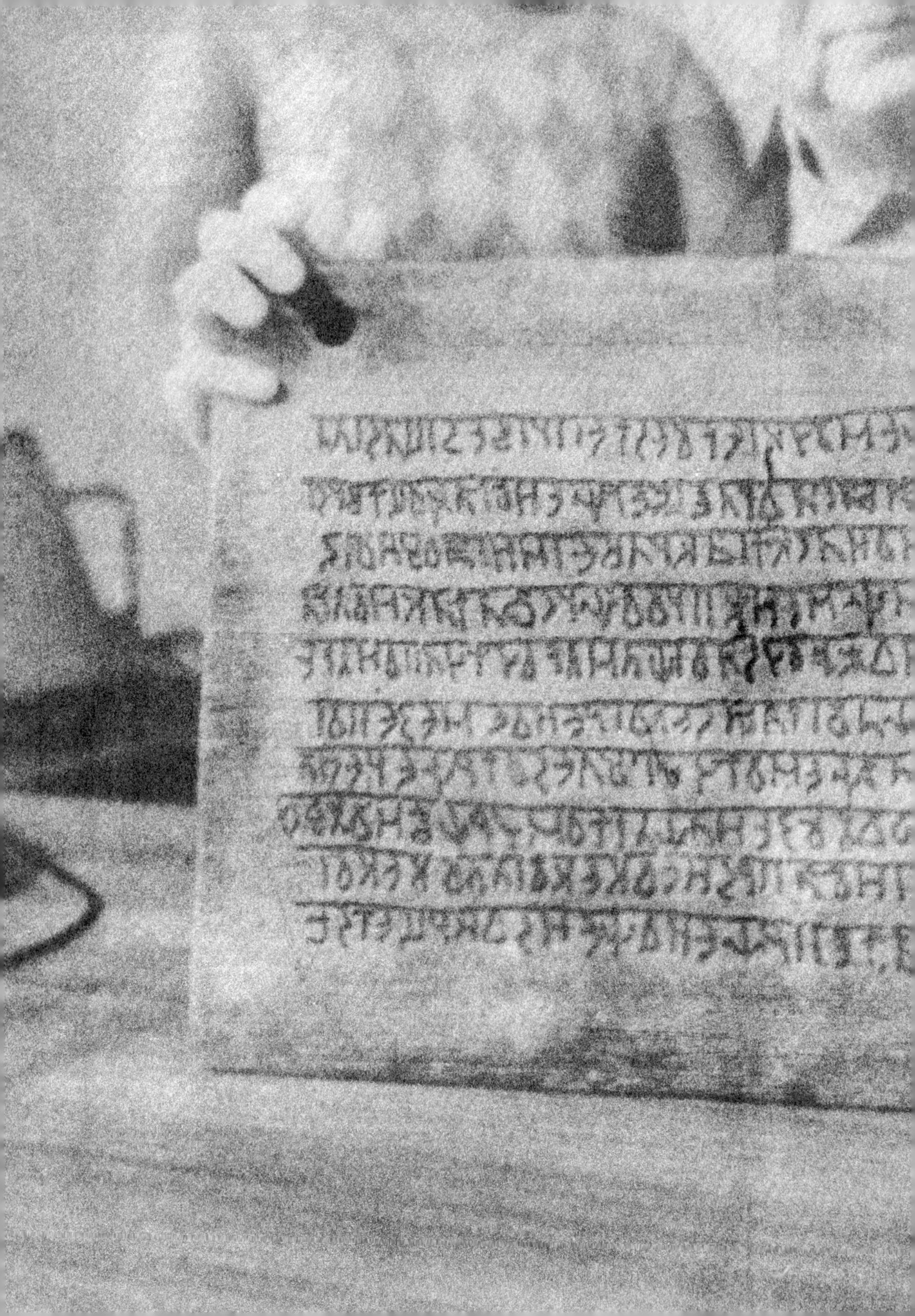

Coordinates:

The city of Veles is the seat of Veles Municipality.

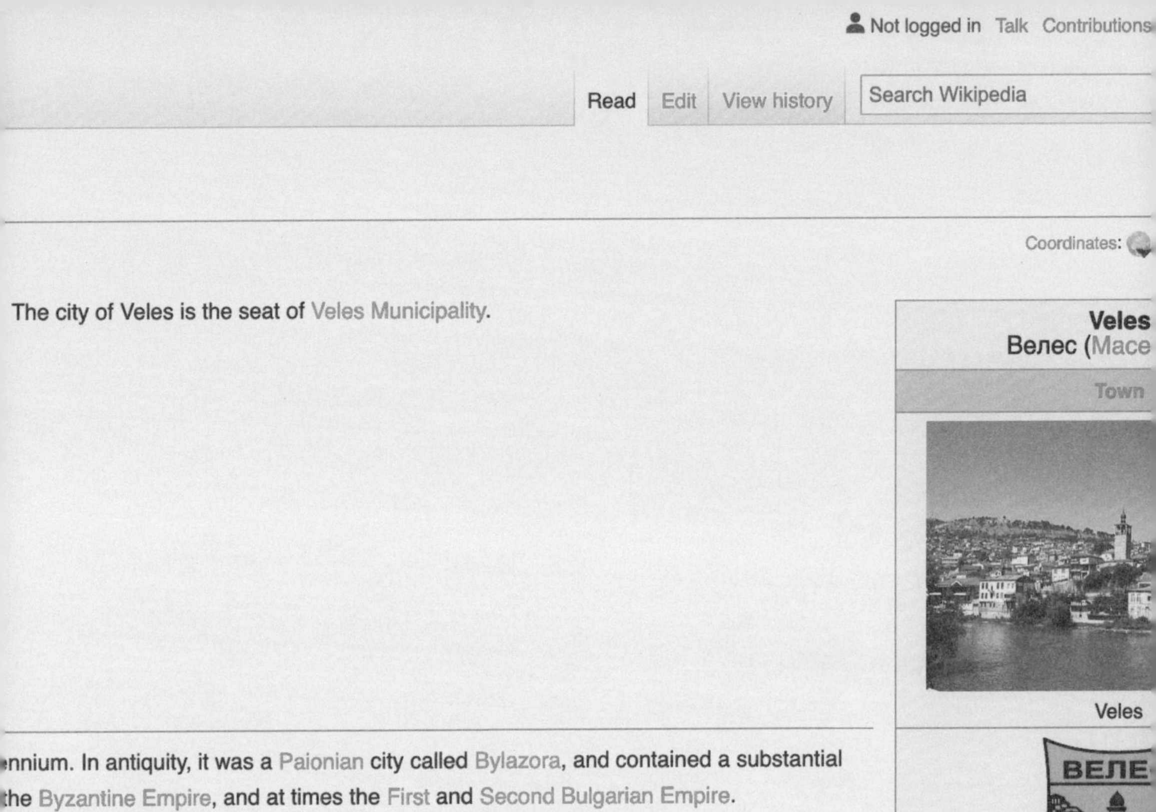

...nnium. In antiquity, it was a Paionian city called Bylazora, and contained a substantial ...the Byzantine Empire, and at times the First and Second Bulgarian Empire.

...rid was bishop.[4][5][better source needed]

...os, Vles)[7] Veles is one of few Slavic gods for which evidence of offerings can be ...rm of a bear) were found in 2003 during excavations of local bronze age gravesites. ...rid was bishop.[4][5][better source needed]

...hiking and camping, especially at the west side of the city. The area is known for its ...arctos arctos).[8][9]

...textile industry, but in the last decades most of the old factories have closed down.

...00 websites producing fake news articles in support of U.S. presidential candidate ...s NewYorkTimesPolitics.com, TrumpVision365.com, USApoliticstoday.com, were ...Veles-based fake news sites were very popular in the months before the 2016 ...ording to media reports, numerous teenagers got rich from their fake news sites.

...sites, but western media reported that numerous Veles-based fake news sites were

Article Talk | Read Edit View history | Search Wikipedia

Book of Veles

From Wikipedia, the free encyclopedia

The **Book of Veles** (also: **Veles Book**, **Vles book**, *Vles kniga*, **Vlesbook**, **Isenbeck's Planks**, Велесова книга, Велесова књига, Велес книга, Книга Велеса, Дощечки Изенбека, Дощьки Изенбека) is a literary epic[1] purporting to be a text of ancient Slavic religion and history supposedly written on wooden planks.

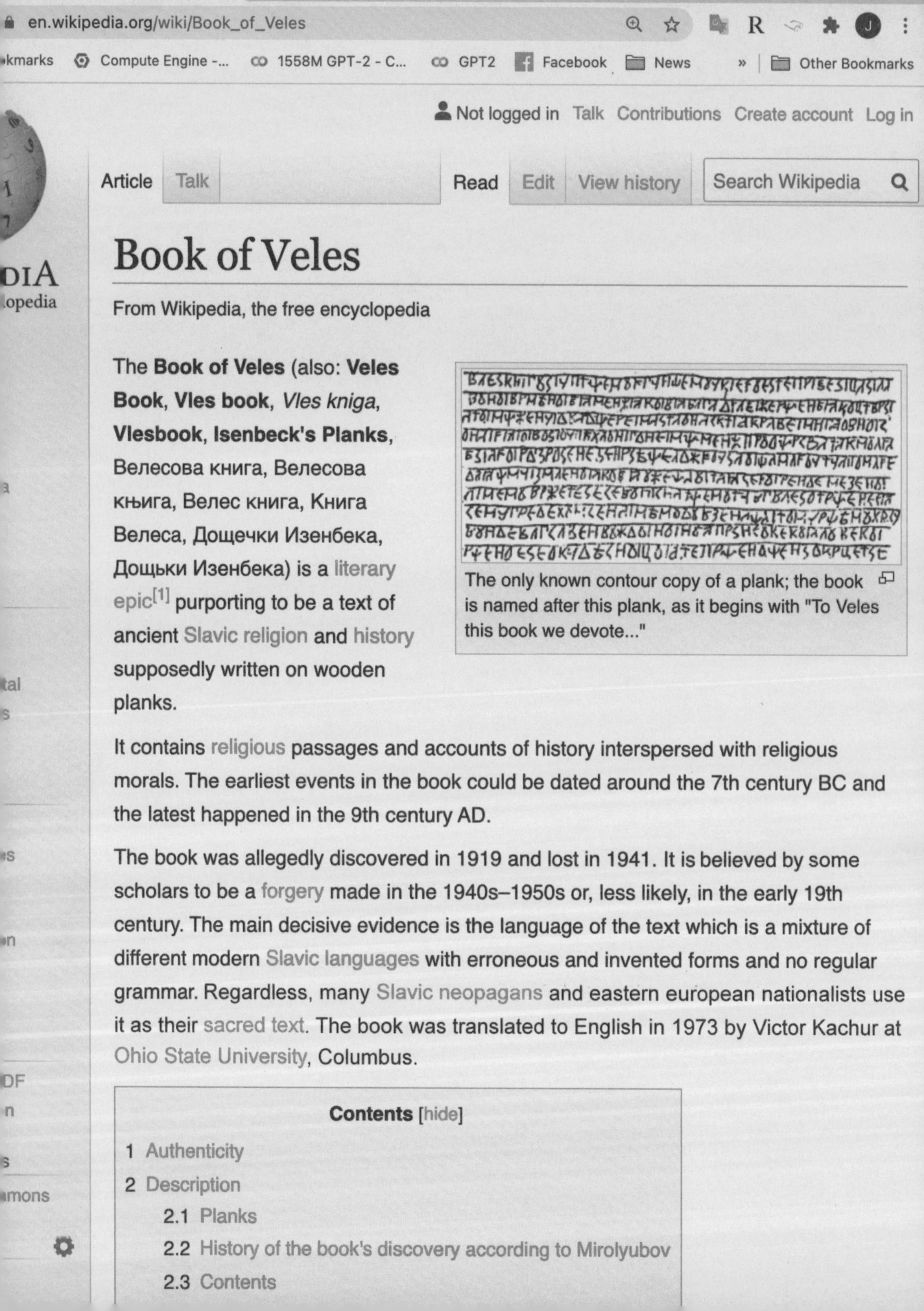

The only known contour copy of a plank; the book is named after this plank, as it begins with "To Veles this book we devote..."

It contains religious passages and accounts of history interspersed with religious morals. The earliest events in the book could be dated around the 7th century BC and the latest happened in the 9th century AD.

The book was allegedly discovered in 1919 and lost in 1941. It is believed by some scholars to be a forgery made in the 1940s–1950s or, less likely, in the early 19th century. The main decisive evidence is the language of the text which is a mixture of different modern Slavic languages with erroneous and invented forms and no regular grammar. Regardless, many Slavic neopagans and eastern european nationalists use it as their sacred text. The book was translated to English in 1973 by Victor Kachur at Ohio State University, Columbus.

Contents [hide]

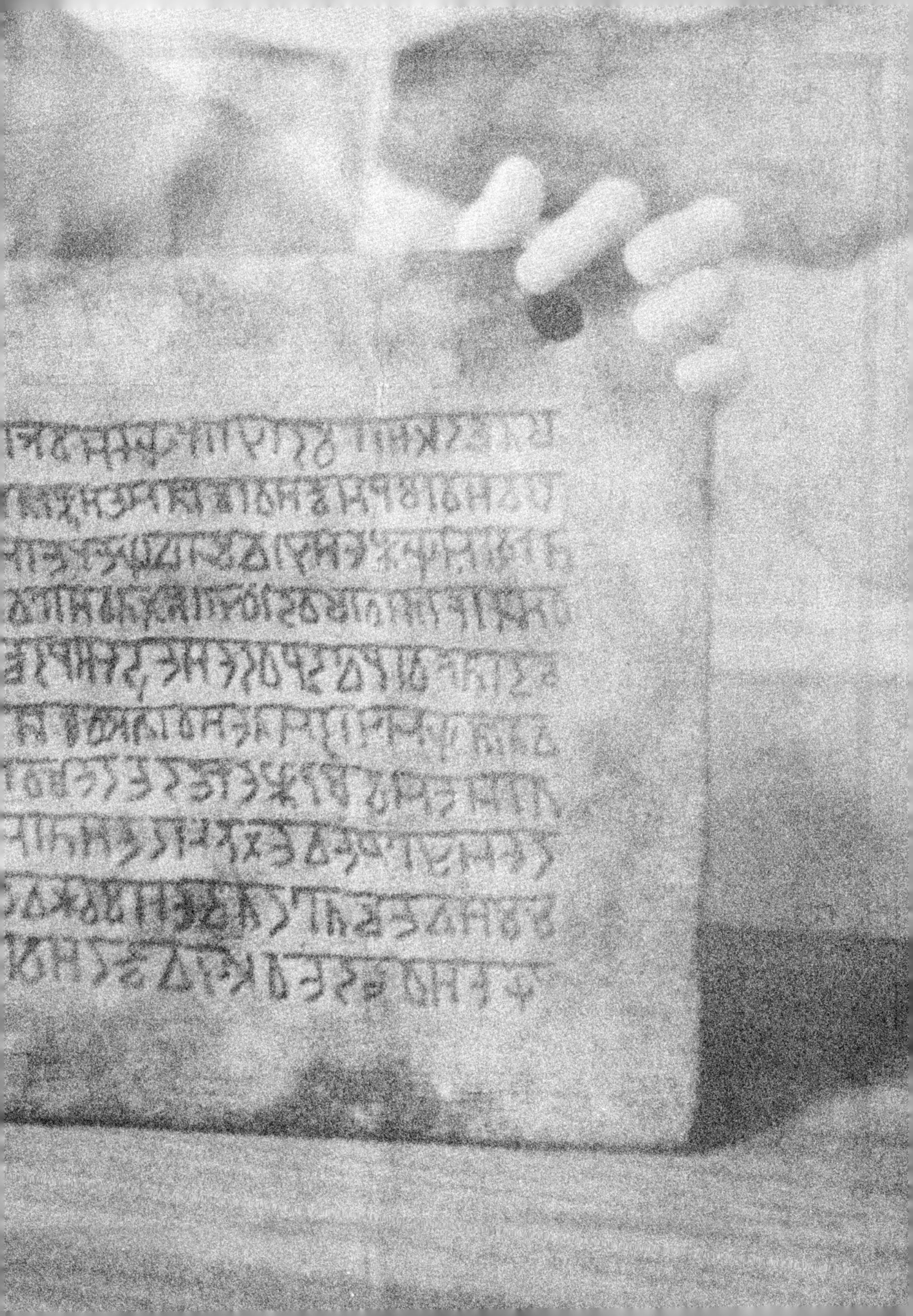

THE BOOK OF VELES

(Vles Knyha)

Key to the History of Eastern Europe (1000 BC to 875 AD)

Copyright 1973 ©

by

Victor Kachur

(Maps and figures from the published reference sources are not included in this copyright.)

Prophetic Writing of Jeremiah (Approximately 600 BC)

"Thus shall ye say unto them:

'The gods that have not made the heavens and the Earth --- these shall perish from the Earth, and from under the heavens'."

Jer. 10:11 The Holy Scriptures (Masoretic Text)

"O Lord, my strength, and my fortress, and my refuge in the day of affliction, the Gentiles shall come unto Thee from the ends of the Earth, and shall say,

'Surely our fathers have inherited lies, vanity, and things wherein there is no profit'. "

Jer. 16:19 The Holy Bible (King James Text)

Additional copies of this publication may be obtained from:

BARAR LOGOS AGENCY
1912 West 73rd Street
Cleveland, Ohio 44102
U S A

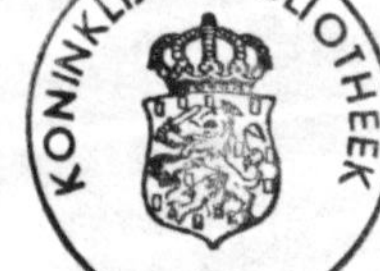

Printed in USA

Miscellaneous Facts and Figures in Lieu of the Foreword

Name of the manuscript: V e l e s is pronounced V-Less.

Time: The time span covered by this manuscript is roughly 1800 years, as shown by the following sampling of dates:

Bohumir	950 BC
Oriy	630 BC
Kie I	650 to 600 BC (?)
Hermanarik	340 to 376 AD
Kie II	473 to 503 AD
Askold	872 to 876 AD.

Date of completion: around 875 AD.

Geography: From Central Asia in the East to Carpathian Mountains in the West; from Novgorod in the North to Egypt in the South.

Importance of the manuscript: Large portions of The Book of Veles present those details of Eastern Europe's history not recorded anywhere else in comparable detail. The manuscript thereby becomes a new source of information about the history, linguistics, religion, ethnology, etc., of Eastern Europe.

When found? 1919.

Where? Somewhere near Kursk, in Russia proper; exact location not determined so far.

Why was The Book of Veles lost?

a) Between 875 and 1919, this manuscript could not be openly studied or published in the newly Christianized Eastern Europe, since it represented a relic of paganism.

b) In addition, the development of two separate Church Slavonic alphabets had made the alphabet used in the manuscript obsolete –– not understood by a casual reader.

c) Low level of education and literacy were generally the rule in Eastern Europe, and higher learning there was oriented mainly for use by the clergy.

Finder: Colonel A. Izenbeck.

Transcriber: Yu. P. Miroliubov.

Original publication: Around 1954 to 1959, in a minor literary magazine (Russian ethnic-language publication in San Francisco, USA).

Original researchers: Yu. P. Miroliubov, A. A. Kur, Prof. S. Paramonov (literary name: S. Lesnoi).

Further publication: 1969-1970, in the Ukrainian ethnic-language publications in Canada.

English translation: The original arrangement of the manuscript has been followed as much as possible when translating its text into English. In some cases the formidable linguistic problems have been by-passed through transliteration. All proper names are generally presented in their original versions; their changing forms provide a clue to the authorship of the separate Boards (chapters) of this manuscript.

Titles: All chapter (Board) titles have been added in translation.

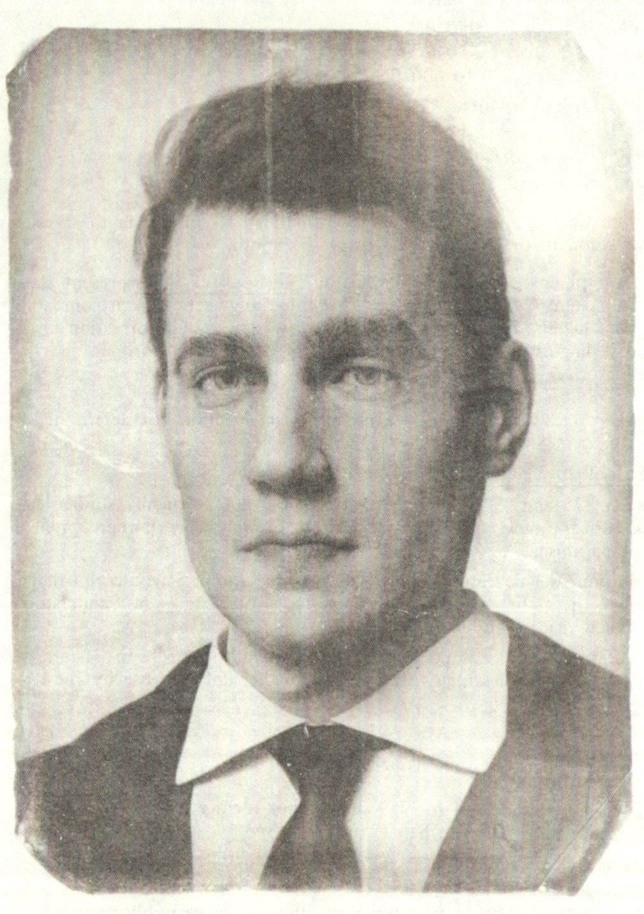

Colonel Fyodor A. Izenbek, discoverer of The Book of Vles

Moscow, 1922. Photographer unknown

APPENDIX I

The Book of Veles:
Discovery and Decipherment

The Book of Veles, a remarkable manuscript dealing with the East European antiquity, was apparently put together from several sources around 875 AD. Its writers were the pagan Rusi (Ruthenes), living in today's Ukraine. Several scribes seem to have been involved, since the manuscript deals with diverse topics, and presents several modifications of the basic writing style.

This "book" had originally been inscribed on thin wooden boards. Each board had a hole for attachment to a leather carrying strap; this served as a rough equivalent of today's book binding.

After 875 AD, no further entries were made. The boards comprising this manuscript had vanished from the view of history. As the long centuries of time went by, this situation served to protect the manuscript from destruction or obliteration. In 988 AD the ruling prince of Ruthene empire, Vladimir (Volodymyr), had accepted the Byzantine Christianity as official state religion. The Book of Veles had somehow escaped the wholesale destruction of pagan writings that followed — probably by being taken to Novgorod in the North, where paganism still managed to hold out.

The decline of Ruthene empire in the Medieval Ages was subsequently followed by the rise of Muscovy to the north -- once but a minor province of the Ruthene lands. The ruling Tsars of Muscovy became also the heirs of the defunct Byzantine Empire in the 15th century. However, education was severely limited in Muscovy to the statesmen and priests.

When Tsar Peter the Great decided to open the cultural communication with the Western Europe, the teaching posts of newly organized universities had to be filled with imported personnel -- largely from Germany. The name of the growing Muscovite Empire became changed to Russia -- a name styled after Prussia.

As the scope of education began to expand, the antiquity of Eastern Europe bagan to emerge from obscurity. Burial mounds from the bygone centuries were excavated. Manuscripts were retrieved, usually from the monasteries; one of these, The Tale of Ihor's Campaign, required a century of dispute to become accepted as a genuine document from the 12th century.

With the coming of World War I, great upheavals convulsed the Russian Empire. In 1919, The Book of Veles had temporarily appeared on the scene. It was found by Colonel A. Izenbeck in the abandoned library of a plundered estate. Colonel Izenbeck, being a former artist attached to archeological expeditions into Asia, immediately recognized the historical nature of the script-covered wooden boards scattered in disorder on the floor. He ordered them to be picked up and taken along. Recalling this incident many years later, Izenbeck was unable to give the location and identity of the estate; it was somewhere near Kursk. His artillery unit had been a part of the Tsarist military expedition into Communist-dominated territory; the unit moved almost daily, in a kaleidoscope of battles. The estate itself had been plundered and burned; its owners were gone — either murdered by the looters, or fleeing for their lives. Their identity remains unknown.

The chronology commonly used in East European historical chronicles gives a count of years "after man"--the creation of man in the Garden of Eden. For example, <u>Nestor's Chronicle</u> and its related manuscripts use the following figures:

From Adam to Noah's Flood	2242 years
From Noah's Flood to Abraham	1082 years
From Abraham to Moses (Exodus in 1487 B.C.)	430 years
From Moses to David	601 years
From David (to Solomon--the early scribes lost 40 years here, and most historians missed this error)	
From the start of Solomon's rule to the captivity of Jerusalem	448 years
From captivity to Alexander	318 years
From Alexander to the birth of Christ (4 B.C.)	333 years

The total in Greek sources is supposed to be 5508 years, while in the Bulgarian sources it is 5500 years; the actual sum of above numbers is only 5454 years, without including the lost 40-year reign of David. The individual year counts up to captivity of Jerusalem are based on the Septuagint translation of the Bible from its Hebrew original into Greek.

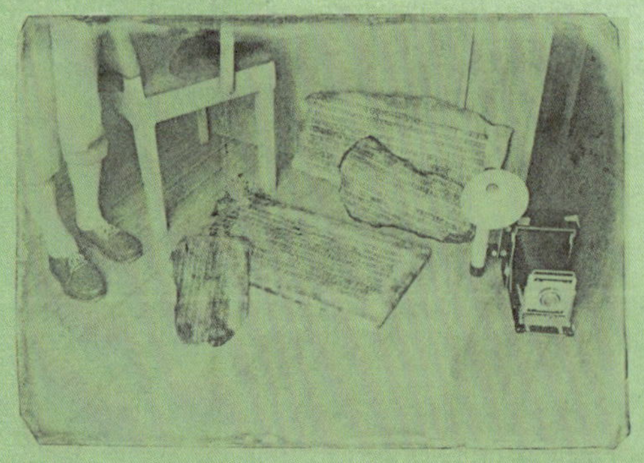

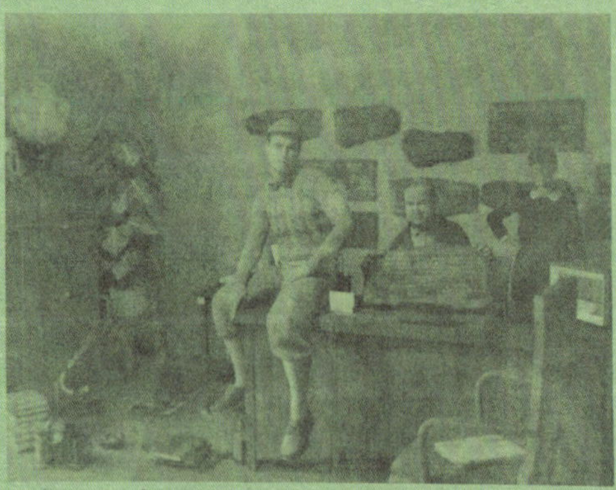

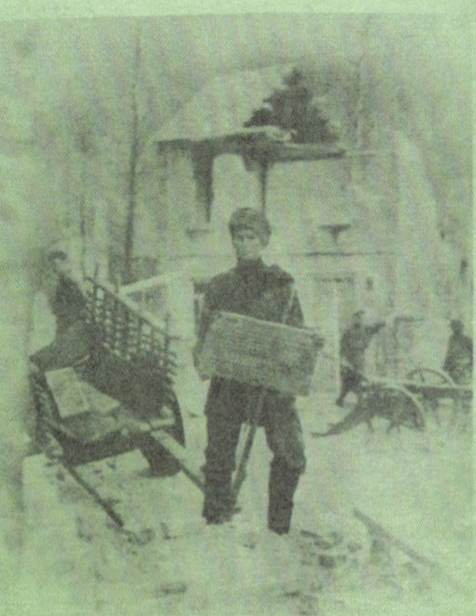

Left, top and bottom:

Izenbeck and Mirolyu-bov with the some of <u>the Book of Veles</u> boards. Brussels, 1928.

Right:

Izenbeck and the boards, soon after the discovery in unknown village, Kursk region, 1919

By 1926, Izenbeck was a refugee in Belgium. He lived in Brussels, and had a good job as an artist with a Belgian firm that specialized in oriental rug-making. The boards of the manuscript were now but a souvenir of war, nearly forgotten and kept out of the way in a dust-covered sack. Izenbeck had realized their impor- tance, but evidently did nothing to discover the exact nature of his find. Further- more, the unintelligible script defied an easy interpretation.

One of Izenbeck's close friends, Mr. Yu. P. Miroliubov, was shown the boards when Izenbeck learned of his plans to write about the past. Miroliubov, a man of some literary talents, thought that he now had a source of original historical mate- rial to provide the background and color for a novel or an epic poem about the bygone days of the Ruthene Empire. He began to work on deciphering the strange script, and soon realized that this was no manuscript like <u>The Tale of Ihor's Cam- paign</u>; instead, it was a far older document.

Working in his spare tiem, Miroliubov spent some fifteen years on <u>The Book of Veles</u>. First the strange alphabet and the solid script-filled lines had to become familiar to the eye, since they were unlike those of the known manuscripts from Eastern Europe. Only occasional words could be separated at first from the unin- telligible background. The ancient Slavic language was dissimilar from the old Church Slavonic that came to be used in the Ruthene Empire after the introduction of Byzantine Christianity.

Working patiently and slowly, Miroliubov spent years to work out the alpha- bet, and to break up the solidly filled script lines into individual words. He could not communicate his discovery until the major part of the manuscript had been deciphered and translated into modern Russian. By that time the Second World War had begun, interrupting the work.

Izenbeck died in 1941, during the war. In the midst of German occupation of Belgium, the original boards had disappeared. Being a bachelor, Izenbeck had no family to look after his belongings. He had not entrusted the original boards to Miroliubov, but merely allowed him to make photographs and to copy the original script in longhand.

After the war, all that Miroliubov had were some photographs, and his exten- sive notes. Even then not all of the original boards had been copied and translated.

<u>The Book of Veles</u> was finally introduced to the public from 1954 to 1959, though on a small scale. Miroliubov had seen a brief notice about the manuscript in a Russian literary magazine being published in San Francisco by the Russian refugees. The writer of this notice, who gave his literary name as A. A. Kur, had asked if anyone knew of the ancient manuscript reputed to be from the pagan Ruthenia (not to be confused with Russia). Miroliubov replied in a lengthy letter that he was the original researcher, and submitted some descriptive details.

Kur became interested in studying the manuscript. Miroliubov eventually left Belgium to come to San Francisco to join him. Between them they began to publish the translations from the individual boards in <u>Zhar-Ptitza</u> (<u>The Fire- Bird</u>), the above-mentioned literary magazine. However, the small circulation of this largely mimeographed magazine did not result in any wide publicity for the manuscript. <u>The Book of Veles</u> thus remained largely unknown even to the special- ists in East European history.

Miroliubov had brought his extensive notes, together with some photographs of the original boards, to San Francisco. After his death they became the property of Kur, who evidently hid them for safekeeping. Thus only the published text became available for the interested researchers.

The first detailed investigation of The Book of Veles appears to have been made by Prof. Paramonov. He had examined the manuscript – largely as presented by Kur and Miroliubov — from a historical viewpoint, and published several books on the progress of his studies. Of these, none were in English; three of the books were in Russian, and one in Ukrainian. Professor Paramonov's death in 1968 terminated his studies before the entire manuscript had been evaluated. His books provide a detailed extension of East European history past the "literacy barrier" of the Ruthene Empire's origins around 900 AD.

Initial studies of The Book of Veles had shown that it deals mainly with the geographical area of Ukraine, south of the Russia proper (old Muscovy). However, the first Ukrainian to obtain a copy of the manuscript had received it only in 1967; he was Mr. M. Skrypnyk, owner of a small publishing establishment in the Hague, Holland.

Having obtained photocopies of the Kur-Miroliubov text, Skrypnyk had quickly communicated with Mr. A. Kyrpych in England about translating the language of the manuscript into modern Ukrainian. This translation was finished early in 1968. The final version appeared as a small, mimeographed booklet called Vles-Knyha (The Book of Veles).

Late in 1969 the text of this booklet was published in two Ukrainian ethnic-language newspapers in North America — the Kanadiyskyi Farmer (Canadian Farmer) in Canada, and Vil'nyi Svit (the Free World) , its associated edition in United States. These newspapers carried The Book of Veles as a serial in their literary section, presenting both the original version of the manuscript and its translation into modern Ukrainian side by side. This entire text of The Book of Veles was then included in the 1970 edition of Canadian Farmer Annual, the Ukrainian ethnic-language almanac..

The Book of Veles thus had reached a larger number of readers. However, its unusual history has made it a subject of controversy. For example, a recently published book in the Soviet Russia makes a brief mention of the manuscript, calling it a forgery from the 19th century; no proof is given as to how this conclusion was reached, while the contents of the manuscript itself are not divulged to the Soviet readers.

The interest in The Book of Veles as a historical document has been largely hampered by the lack of its translation into English. The translation of the manuscript's text into English has been undertaken in this preprint publication to provide this major document of East European antiquity for further studies.

N. SKRIPNIK
P.O. Box 95936
2509 CX The Hague
The Netherlands

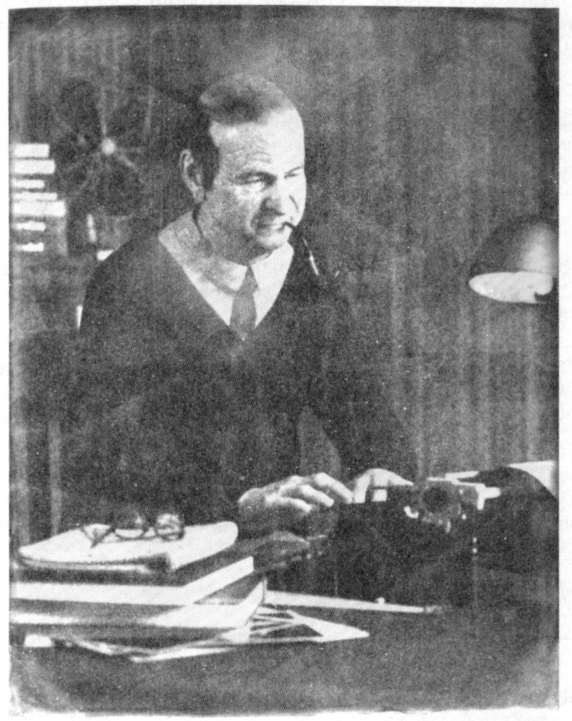

Yuri Miroliubov, at work in his study. Brussel, Belgium, date
unknown. Photo by Natascha Miroliubov.

Board 2 - B

(Note: The text continues from Board 2-A)

(...) here we will build a fortress-town (ΓPADIE)".

And it was a great city, with a fame acknowledged all around by the people, who went to see it. And from it came forth lies, and became famous.

For the house of Veles (BΛEC) will be our fortress, and the wall will be broken down. And with our swords we will pierce it, and then perish. But here the god of this world uses his power to deceive. When he comes to us in the flesh, he lies and steals.

Thus that famous city was abandonded by them. And it is related from the ancient time that we have to be on guard - lest the enemy come upon us, and we should be washed away by them. Nowadays is another time, and we have to take hold of the bridle, and to pull forward.

***

Thus it was that Matr Sva (MATP CBA) beats her wings, and sings the songs of combat. And that bird is not the Sun, but she comes from it, and such she was meant to be, and we must follow her.

And we see in the sky a star like the sun, and a fiery cloud. And from the fiery cloud comes a forth a column of lightening. But the Matr Sva Slava (MATP CBA CΛBA) went behind them, and thus led them to the junction of the Tiverts and the Danube (ΔAHAE)rivers. And there they (...)

(Note: This Board is much shorter than the others – possibly through incomplete transcription.)

Historical Note:

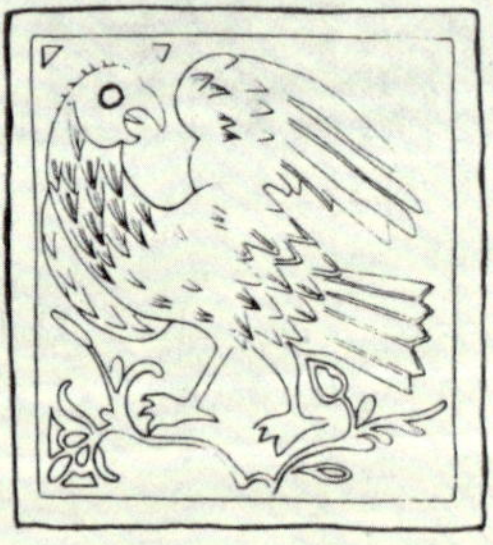

Falcon

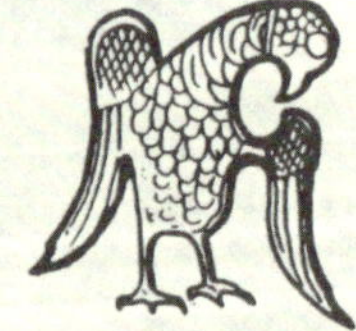

Bird of Victory

The Bird of Victory (called the Matoir Sva Sl[a]va Bird in the text) was probably patterned after the common falcon or hawk. The picture of the falcon given above represents a sample of the monastery art near Moscow, from the Middle-Age Europe. Historical authenticity of the Bird of Victory in The Book of Veles has been confirmed by the latest research on the heraldry symbols of Riurikovichi princes.

Source: Slaviane i Rus' (The Slavs and Ruthenia), in Russian, Nauka Publishing House, Moscow, 1968.

Falcon: page 464   Bird of Victory: page 217

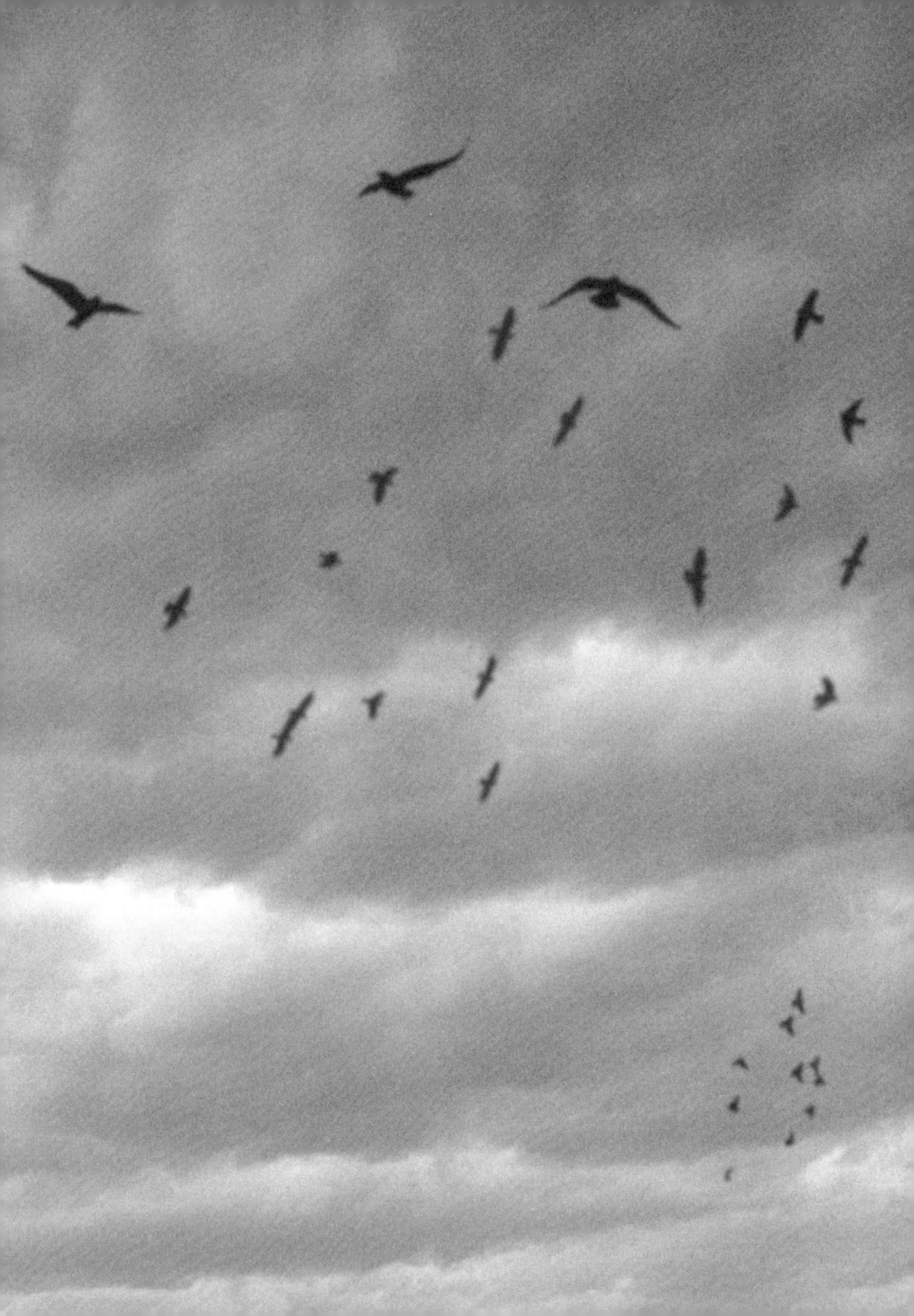

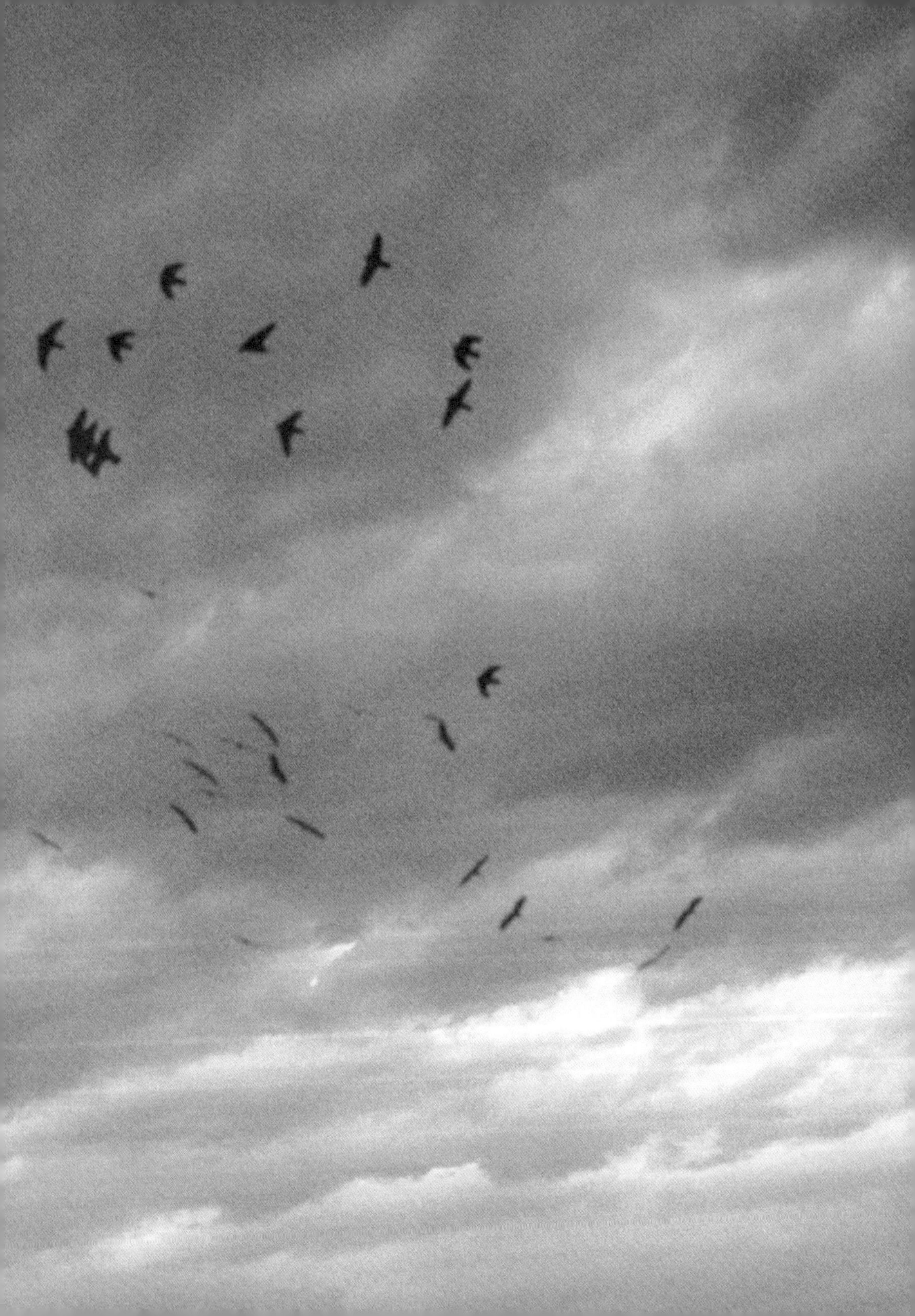

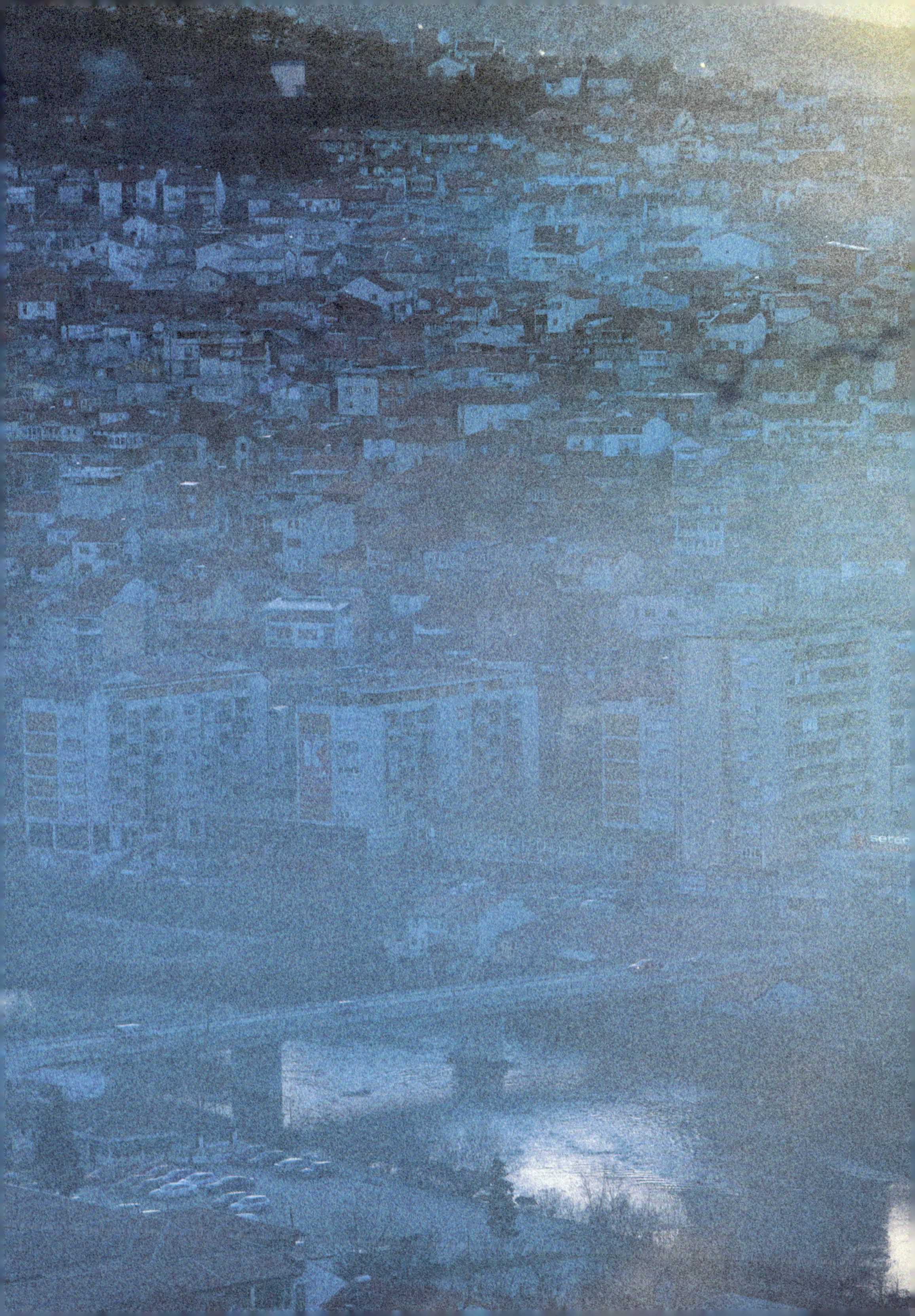

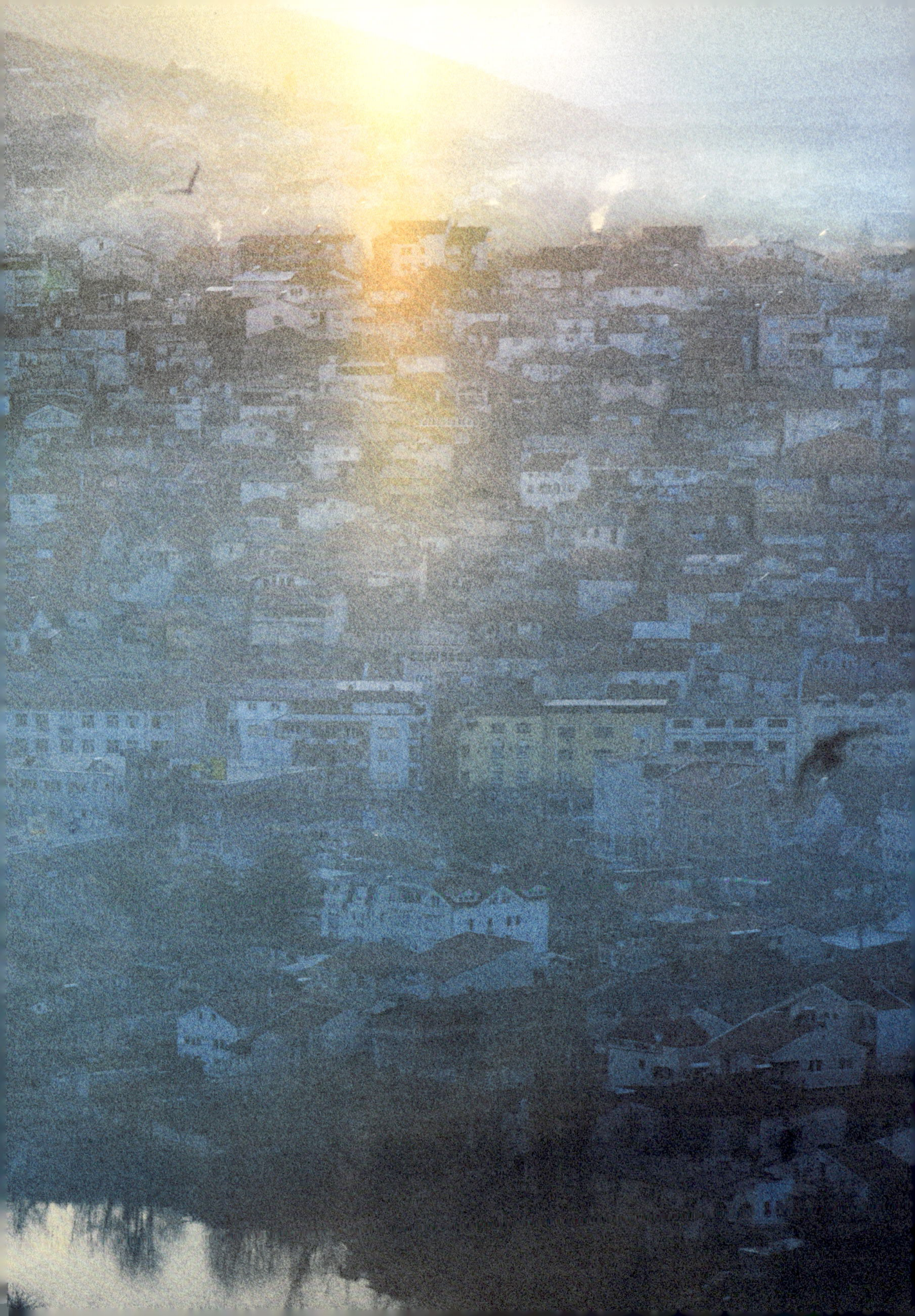

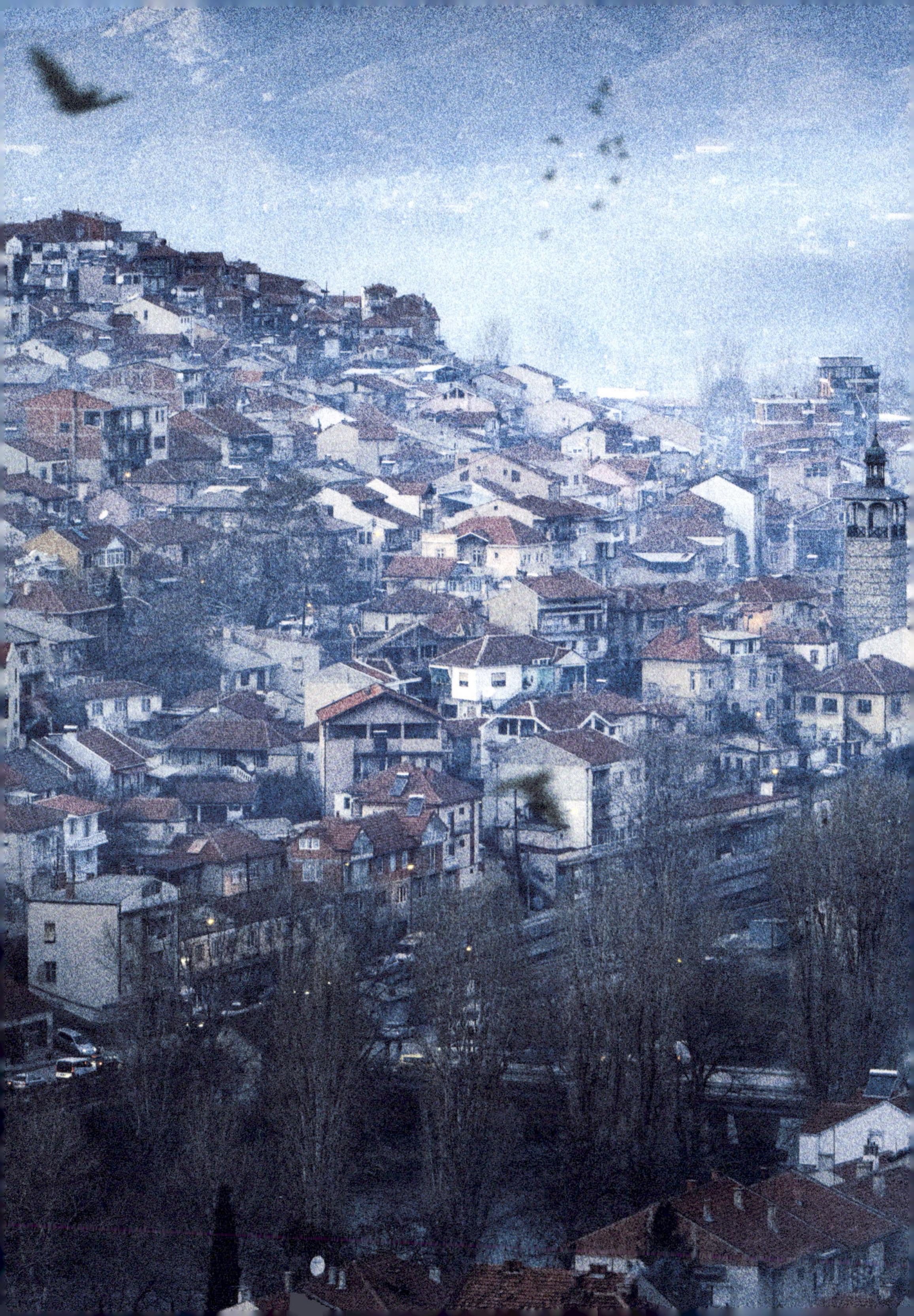

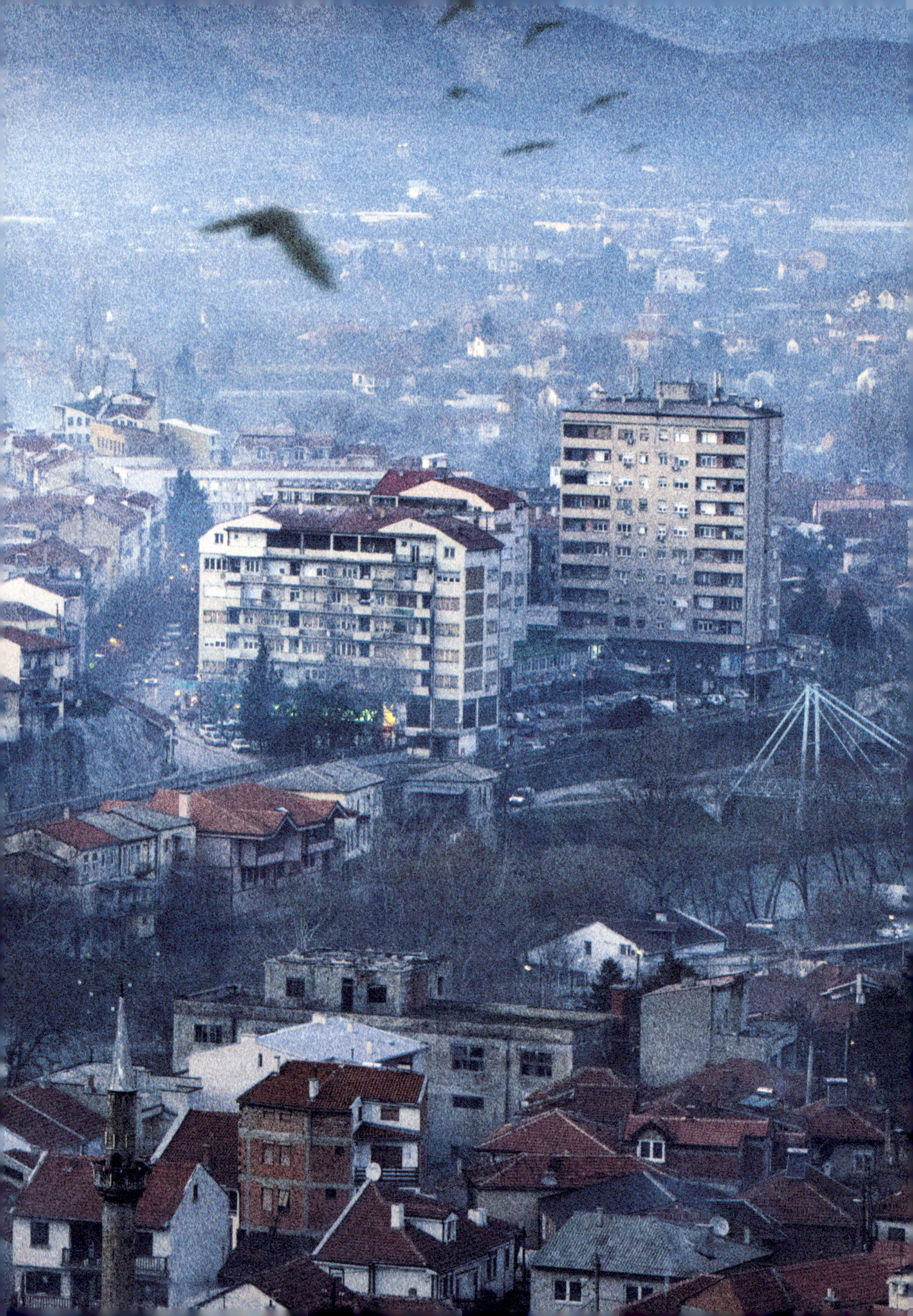

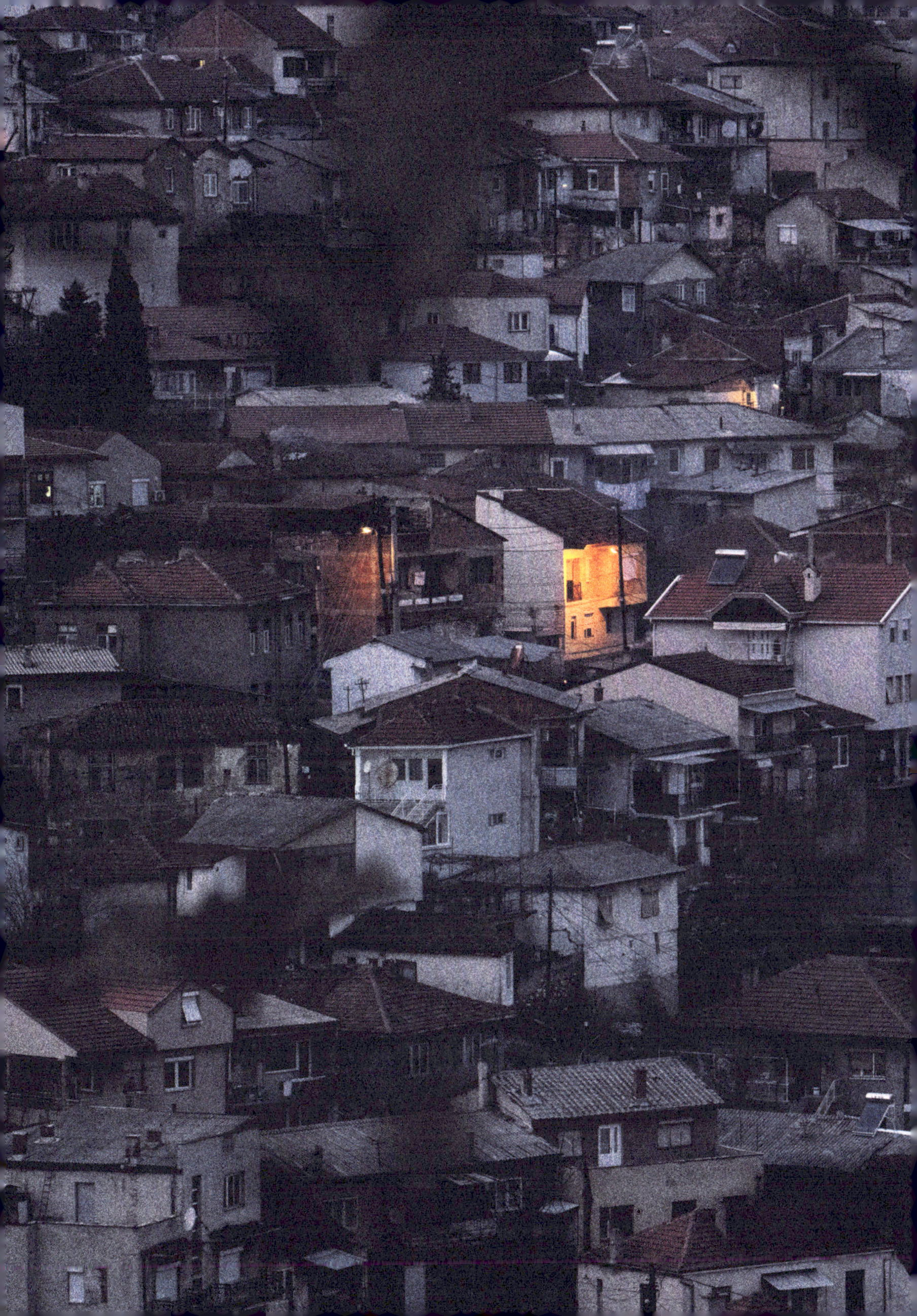

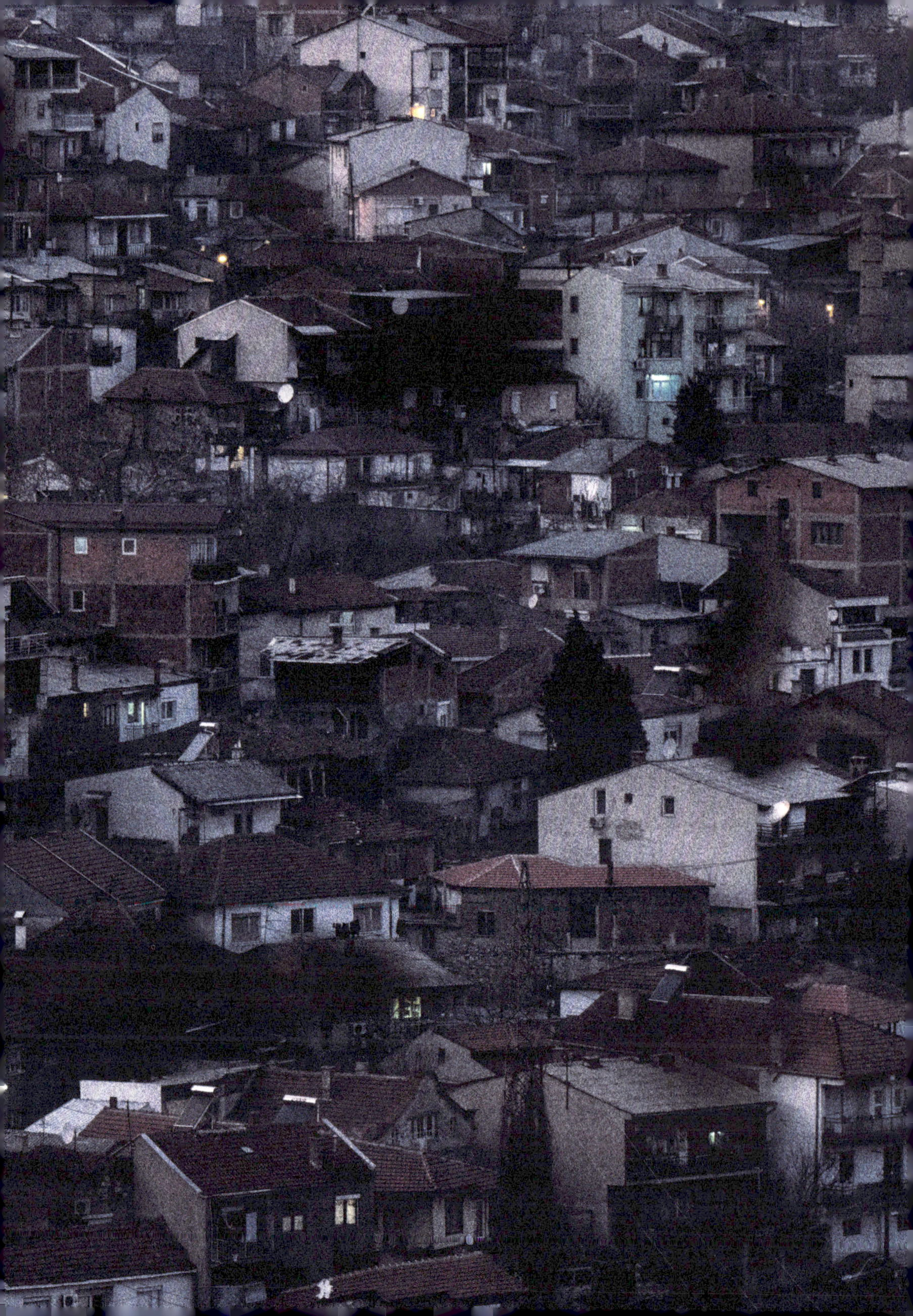

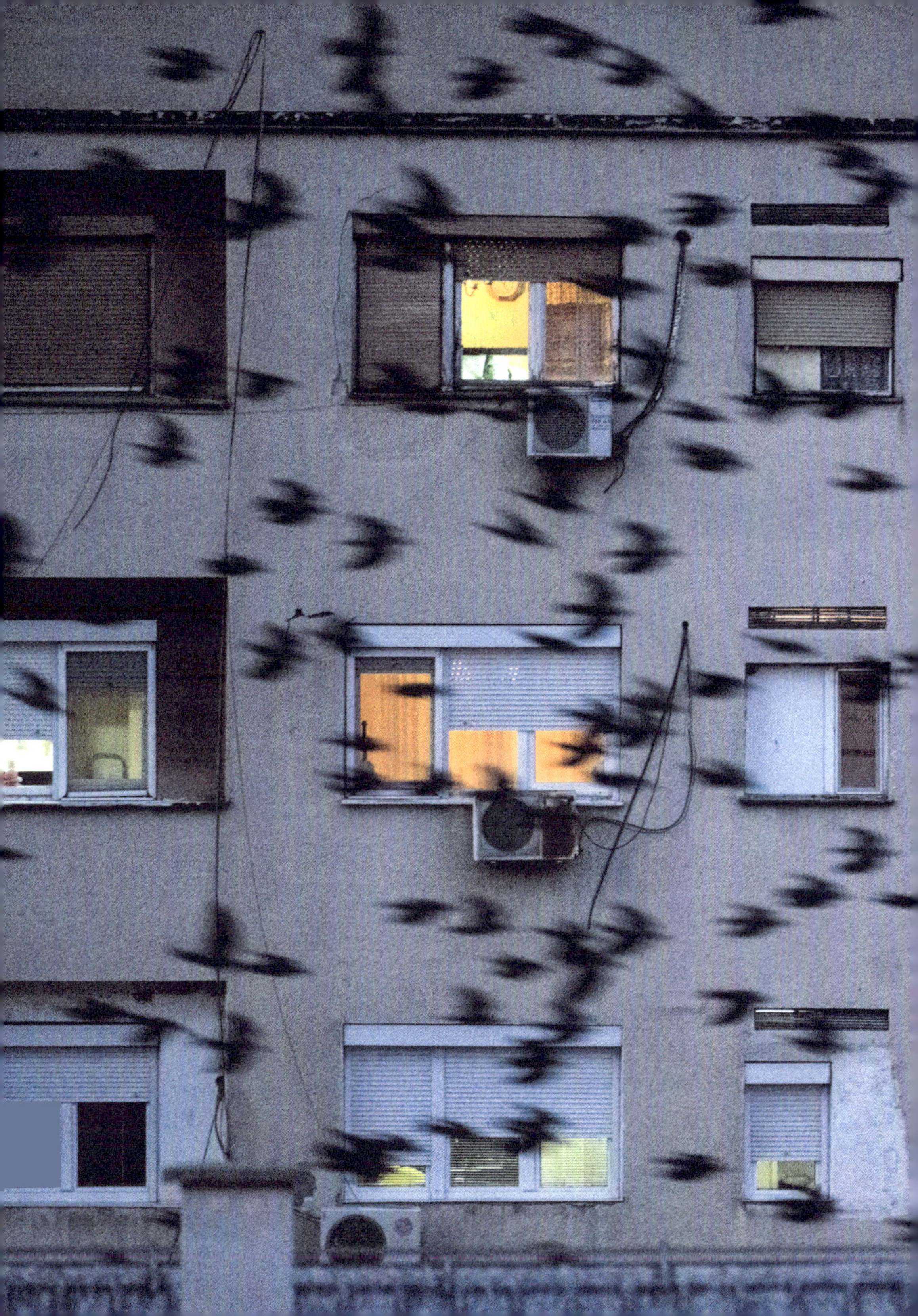

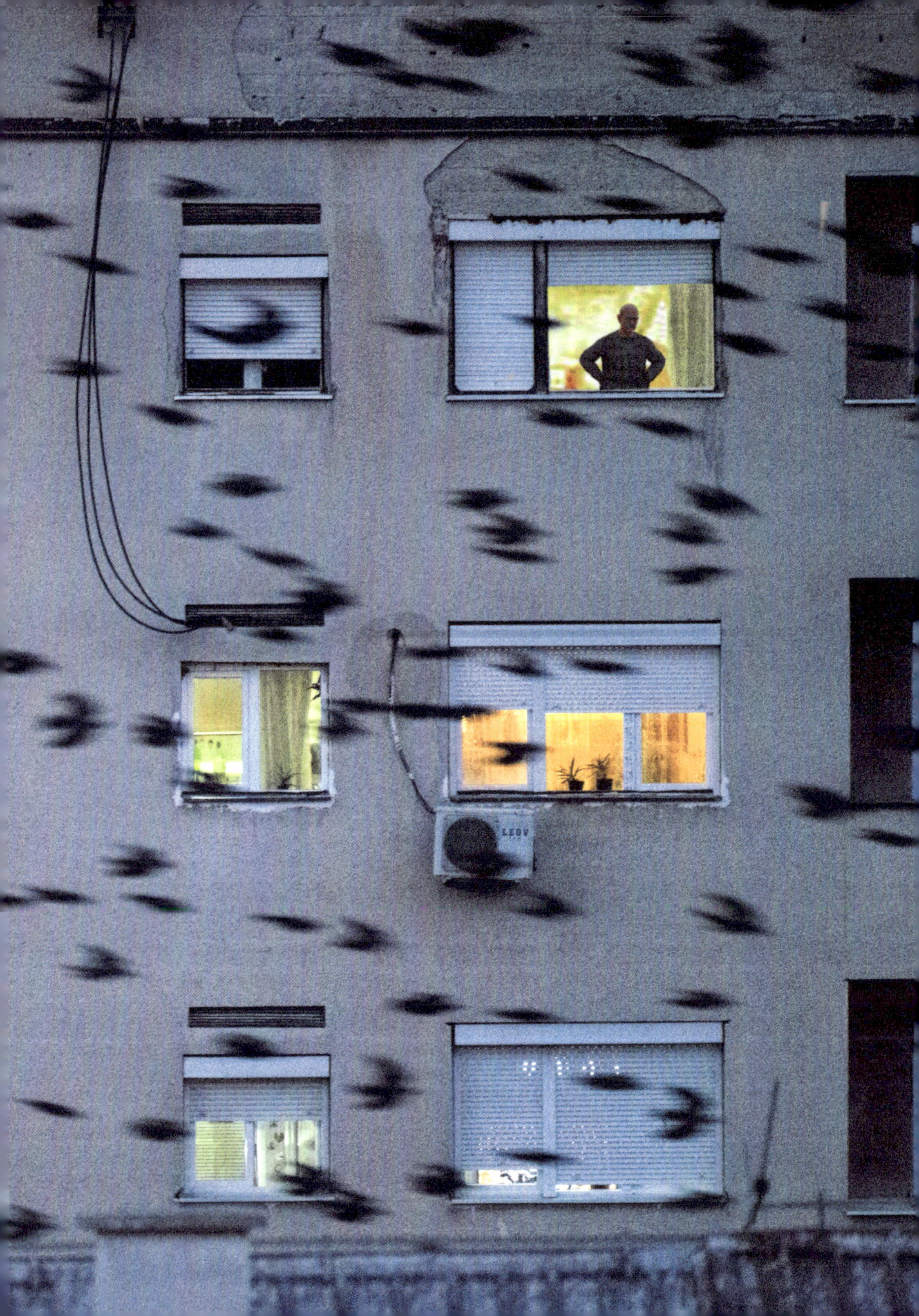

THE BOOK OF VELES

JONAS BENDIKSEN

GOST

IN 2016, VELES
BECAME THE MECCA
OF THE POST-FACTUAL ERA.
WHAT WAS ONCE
A MANUFACTURING HUB
IN THE FORMER YUGOSLAVIA
IS NOW HOSTING
A COTTAGE INDUSTRY
EXPORTING FAKE NEWS
TO UNSUSPECTING
AMERICANS.
HOW DID A TOWN
THAT USED TO PRODUCE
CLOTHING AND CHINA
NOW HOUSE THOUSANDS
OF FAKE NEWS WEBSITES?

I have been a photojournalist for more than twenty years and have travelled around the world, covering everything from the war in Afghanistan to the refugee crisis in Europe. I have also been a journalist in the Balkans, where I've worked for more than a decade. I'm not a journalist who uses fake news. I use my camera to tell stories, not to make them. But, when it comes to the fake news, I have always been fascinated by it.

I want to tell people about the fake news industry. The fake news industry is very powerful and it is very dangerous. I think that if we don't fight it, we will be very sorry. It was an interesting journey. I got to know people who worked for fake news sites, who had a lot of experience in the business, who were actively trying to make money from fake news. I also interviewed journalists and experts from the fake news industry, and learned a lot about what is going on in that world. This is a story about how the fake news industry works.

I arrived in Veles in the early afternoon of June 3. Upon arrival, I found the mayor, a man named Diokno, sitting in his office. Diokno is a tall, thin man with a large mustache and a bald head. He was wearing a black suit and tie and was surrounded by his staff. I asked him about the state of the city. He told me that the city was in a state of complete collapse. He had been mayor for twenty years and had never seen anything like it.

The mayor told me that the city had been a major industrial center for more than a hundred years but that over the last decade, the economy had been destroyed. The factories that had once employed thousands of people had all closed. Now, the city was simply a collection of abandoned buildings. According to the mayor, 50% of young Macedonians are unemployed.

A few years ago, Veles was the capital of a booming, modern, and cosmopolitan city. It was the center of a major pharmaceutical manufacturing plant and a major hospital complex. But today, the city is a ghost town. The city's main airport, the main manufacturing facility, and the hospital have all closed. The city is littered with empty buildings and crumbling, decrepit structures.

I start walking through the city. It's not beautiful. The streets were empty. I knew the Macedonian economy was in decline, but I didn't know it had reached a point of no return. The only sign of life was a few poorly-lit kiosks selling snacks and drinks. Empty factories, once bustling with activity, were replaced by lifeless patches of asphalt.

Five minutes' walk down a deserted highway from the city center, I noticed a BMW 4 Series parked by the side of the road. I asked the driver what was on her mind. After some back and forth, she and her friends agreed that the most pressing issue facing the country was unemployment.

Many factories had been shuttered, and with it, factory jobs. Its sole functioning hospital was closed a few years ago, and its downtown withered. Many young people had left the town to seek greener pastures elsewhere. No factory or office was left standing, and the local soccer team, Dnepr, had been dropped from the first division to the third.

But a miracle happened in the town of 50,000 people—the opening of a new era. The disappearance of good paying jobs has also created a thriving black market for low-quality fake news. The fake news industry is a perfect example of how the internet has transformed our world. More than 100 prominent US politics websites were registered in Veles, most created within the last twelve months. These sites tend to follow recognizable patterns: they follow news about Trump, often blatantly plagiarizing and sensationalizing it.

The fake news houses in Veles have become rich from two events: the 2016 US presidential election and the Brexit vote. BuzzFeed said it had spoken with people who worked on the sites and found them to be "well-run, highly organized, and highly productive". The Facebook gold rush has certainly provided work for locals. Many of them were young people struggling to make a living. They just didn't know how much money they could make in fake news.

I spoke with a sixteen-year-old fake news creator in Veles who created several social media profiles in support of American politics. He says he now employs three to five people, including two teenagers, all working together to deliver high quality, viral content. They launch posts around midnight, and then disappear for a day or two, reading new tweets from their followers. Then they post about what they just saw, hoping to grab some new shares. Then they go back to tweeting about Trump.

"I live alone and do not have any relatives to care for me. My stepbrother works in a factory, my stepmother works in a textile company, my uncle owns a small house, my cousins all work in the same factories. I have been forced to work two or three jobs just to survive. I live in poverty here in Macedonia. We earn about 200-300 euros monthly for a family of three. My dad works in a chemical company, so I have always been interested in technology."

"I worked on Trump's campaign from the beginning. I was paid about 200 a month for a job which involved finding stories which would make the Trump campaign look good. The whole thing was just a big way of making money, using social media to spread the word. It was the most powerful thing that has ever happened to my life. Because of this, my life has changed forever. I tried to write what people wanted to read. I don't think they believed all the lies I was writing, they were just buying into the stories I was presenting."

What is certain is that the perpetrators of the fake news business knew how the system worked. Among the most successful US politics sites was Marco's. It launched in June 2016 and has been described as the world's most successful fake news site. It now has more than 310,000 Facebook followers, according to Facebookintelligence.com.

It was getting late afternoon when

I met up with Marco in a café in Skopje. It was raining, so I decided to walk around to some other places in the city, like the Opera House or the Belvedere Theatre. When I got there, Marco pointed his finger at a map in his hand. It was from his website, which he runs with a partner. It showed that the Veles sites had more than two million Facebook followers, which is something Marco doesn't want to think about. He prefers to think about his site as a full-service hotel chain, with every detail prepared and ready to go.

He showed me his website. By now it had secured $60,000 in revenue, a sizable sum in a country where the average monthly salary is $371. Backed by Google AdSense, it purports to have nearly eight million followers, mostly in the US.

The Macedonian crisis began when the country's Prime Minister, Nokola Gruevski, ordered the Macedonian army to stop taking part in the NATO military alliance, which had been instrumental in supporting the NATO-led peacekeeping operations in Bosnia and Kosovo.

Gruevski's refusal to participate in the NATO operation in Libya led to a massive anti-government protest movement in the streets of Macedonia, which culminated in the toppling of the government in February. The Macedonian crisis reached a peak when the Macedonian army began to take part in the NATO-led military operations in Libya. The European Union imposed severe economic sanctions on the country.

The city of Veles had been prosperous for over a century, but in recent years the people had begun to lose their confidence in the city. They were not sure of the future. I saw the signs of this decay everywhere. There were abandoned buildings, with broken windows and doors. The roads were littered with the detritus of abandoned vehicles.

I met a man who told me he had come to the city from Greece on foot. He had been unable to find work and had been homeless for two months. He said he was a teacher, and that he had been forced to leave his family in Greece because they were too poor to feed him. He had been staying with friends in Veles, but he said that they had refused to help him. He was now sleeping on the streets.

However, the largest single source of income for the town of 60,000 is from its thriving fake news industry. I was surprised to find out that the fake news industry is one of the main sources of income for the people of Veles. According to the Macedonian Ministry of Economic Development, the fake news industry generated around $2.1 billion in 2016. Fake news has a direct impact on the country's economy.

I drove around the tired streets of Veles. Run-down neighborhoods, empty shops, and abandoned factories dominated the skyline. I stopped in front of a small, white, three-story building. The main entrance was broken off by a pile of rubble. Small-time drug dealers and pirates roamed the seedy interiors. How could this place be so lifeless, I thought, nothing could be salvaged from this place; this junk food town, this fake news town. Nobody wanted to work here anymore.

I parked my car near the entrance of the building and walked up the steps to the front door. There was a sign on the door that said, "Welcome to the Fake News Factory."

I had a good feeling about this. I walked into the building, and there it was: the office of a fake news agency. It was a small room with a desk and a computer. The windows were covered with black plastic, and there were no lights. There was a small wooden table with a lamp and a laptop.

I sat down on the table, and a young man with dark hair and a face that looked like it had been painted with a black marker sat down next to me. "Welcome to the Daily News," the young man said. "I'm your host, and I'll be your translator. In the next few minutes, we'll be discussing some of the events that have taken place in Veles over the past few days." I nodded.

Goran was an internet troll. He had dark hair that was parted in the middle, and was dressed in jeans, a t-shirt, and a hoodie. He was a young man of average height, with a clean-shaven face and a very friendly and outgoing personality. Goran's social media presence was very strong. He had a lot of followers. He was always in a dark room with his headphones on. He would hang out on a popular Discord server with a group of other trolls. The server was called "Echo of Veles".

Goran was not a native of Veles. He had a lot of skills, he was a good writer, he was a good hacker. Goran was one of the most powerful trolls in Veles, and he was capable of manipulating people into doing anything he wanted.

He was a part of the group that would play music and make memes. He would also play other games, such as "World of Warcraft", and "Dota 2". He also had a YouTube channel that he used to make funny videos. Goran was very outgoing, and he was also very popular with girls. Goran's main role in the Veles campaign was to troll and spread fake news.

"We post fake news for a living. A good chunk of the world doesn't know that we exist, so we earn a good living. Fake news is the number one click-bait source on the net. There are too many haters on the net. I have to choose between hating Hillary or supporting Trump. Which one do you think I am more attached to? I am fully aware that I am supporting a political candidate, but I am also fully aware that I am supporting a business. I work really hard to support my family. I started with just a few fake news sites and have since added a lot more. My main motivation is making money from this. I want to give back to my country and make money for my kids. The more people know about Trump, the easier it will be to make money out of this business. My political posts are the same as anyone else's political posts, I'm simply using Facebook to share my own views and to spread the word around."

The majority of the fake news we read on social media is written by young people. The internet is their world, so they are the first ones to say things that the rest of us will not think twice about. The internet is their language. The problem is that most of the things that are written on the internet are fake. The only thing that is not fake is the internet itself. The fake news industry is based on two main pillars: the distribution of misinformation via social media platforms, and the dissemination of "news" through mainstream media outlets. The spread of fake news is facilitated by the use of bots, which are automated online software programs that are used to spread misinformation.

I spoke to Trump supporter Alex, a thirty-four-year-old dental hygienist in Veles. It's important to understand that the people who are writing the news for Trump sites are not even remotely interested in informing the public. They are only pursuing profit.

He and his friends "work" around the clock, posting news, photos, and engaging with their followers. "I support Trump for a few reasons. One, he makes money. Two, he makes Americans happy. Third, he makes money quickly."

"Nobody can stop us, not even the police. There are too many haters on the net, and too many fake news sites, and fake news is the new truth. The main thing is that we believe in freedom of speech." He goes on to say, "People are born with certain biases," however, he doesn't think that those biases are malicious, they are just human. When I ask him if he believes that humans are inherently evil, he doesn't think that they are. "They are just tools."

Confirmation bias means people tend to look for information they can use to reinforce their own prejudices. When people see information that fits their own point of view, their brain tells them that the story is real, and the people in the story are real.

I was told by a local that, "You have to understand that the economy is the most important thing here, the politics is secondary. If they have a bad economy, it doesn't matter what kind of politician is in power, they will just throw more money at the problem."

This was not the case. The economy was in a crisis, the media was in a state of crisis. And the politician in power was the one who had the most money, who had the most connections, and who had the most people behind him.

I met with the mayor, a member of the ruling party, and a few other people who were involved in the fake news industry. The mayor was a very nice man, but he was very reluctant to talk about the industry. He wanted to avoid the topic because he thought it was too controversial. He said that the fake news industry was an illegal industry, that it is illegal to make false information, and that the government would prosecute people who were involved in the fake news.

The mayor said that there was a fake news business in Veles, but that he didn't know how much money was made. I asked him what kind of fake news was being made in Veles. He said that fake news is not just fake news. There is also fake news about football, about politics, about celebrities, and about everything.

He said that he didn't know exactly how much money was made in Veles, but that it was "a lot." The fake news industry is the biggest source of income for this small town. The mayor of Veles, the most influential person in the town, is a Russian citizen, and he has been accused of being a Russian agent.

I asked the mayor how the fake news industry worked. He said that it was very simple. People would take an article that had been published by a website that was fake and use it as a basis for a fake news story. He said that the fake news industry is very much alive and well in Veles. People are still operating, and they are still making fake news. The mayor said some of the producers had gone as far as impersonating journalists. "There are always going to be people who are going to work for fake news, and there will be people who are going to work for real news," he said. The mayor said some of the young people working for him had embezzled more than $60,000 off their salaries. He said some had stolen identities and were using pseudonyms.

I met up with Bojan and his two friends, both of whom are minors, to find out how they made their fake news videos look professional. He was wearing a green and black striped shirt, jeans and brown shoes. He is one of scores of Macedonian teenagers who are behind a cottage industry in the small city of Veles that's been churning out fake pro-Donald Trump pieces on American politics for some time. He said that he had been involved in the creation of the "Pizzagate" conspiracy theory for more than a year, and that he had been the first one to make it into the mainstream. He was one of the most popular trolls in Veles.

"I taught myself how to make money on the internet," said Bojan, who is eighteen. "I looked at the sources, some were fake, some were real, and I wanted to make sure that everything I was making wasn't fake. Then I joined a team and worked on it together."

He said one of the reasons he became interested in politics is because his parents were both journalists. The reason Bojan was so successful was that he had a reputation for being an excellent hacker. He could hack into any system he wanted, and he was known for being able to compromise and hack into virtually any computer system. He also was very good at creating fake news, and he created many sites, and he was good at creating fake news that was very believable.

"The thing about bots is that they are not real people. They are machines," he continued. "They are not thinking. They are not feeling. They are only doing what they are told to do." The Macedonians who run these sites say they don't care about Mr. Trump. "I have a different idea. How can we live without Trump? How can we live without fake news?" asks Bojan.

The next day I was walking along the outskirts of the city. There were a few old stone buildings and a few small houses which were built by the rich people who were moving into the area. I noticed a group of young men standing around a large bear. The bear was tied up and looking pretty worn out. The men were watching the bear as it stared at them. I was a little surprised at how quiet it was.

The men were a little skeptical. I asked them why they were so scared. They said that the bear had been "taking over their town." They said that the bear was killing their cattle. I asked them what they were going to do. They said they were going to kill the bear. It was a very emotional moment. I didn't know what to say. I just kept thinking "I'm so sorry." I remember the smell of blood, sweat and death.

There are also reports of bears in the country killing people. In the village of Vlach, in northern Macedonia, a man was killed by a bear in 2012. The man was collecting wood, when a bear came out of the woods and attacked him.

The local media has been forced to run stories about them, as they are considered a nuisance. The local TV station was reporting on the wild bears in the area. The newspapers were all reporting on the same story. The bears have been known to attack people who are not used to them. The bears also sometimes eat garbage, and they are not able to digest it.

In 2015, the number of bears in the area was estimated to be about eight hundred. Today, there are around one thousand.

"The problem is that they come to the city to eat garbage and leftovers," says Frantz Mladenovski, a resident of Veles who runs a wildlife rehabilitation center. "They eat the garbage, then they get sick. The disease they get from the garbage is called glanders. It's a contagious disease. It spreads through the air. It's very dangerous."

"The bears are a problem for us," says Mladenovski. "We can't manage them all. We have to look at what we can do. We are trying to find solutions. Many residents of Veles are fed up with the bears. They also feel that the animal is a problem for the local economy. Since the bear is said to be a symbol of power and honor, they are very popular with tourists. However, in 2010 a group of tourists were attacked by a bear near the city. In 2016, the municipality spent about $150,000 to protect Veles from bears."

Mladenovski says that he has seen bears attack children and dogs. "I saw a bear just eating a dog. They are very dangerous."

I decided to go out and see for myself, so I packed my camera. I drove to the nearest village, Kastelu, and met with a local man named Nikoli. I explained that I was a journalist and that I was documenting the situation. He showed me the location of the bears and told me that he had seen the same bears in the area in July and August. I asked him if I could photograph them in the wild, and he said yes. He also said that they were all around the same age, between eight and twelve years old. He said that they were in very good health, and that they were not afraid of humans.

I parked the car and walked into the forest. There were big trees, with big branches. I took a few pictures and then walked a little way down a hill. As I got closer, I could see them, the curious black-and-white animals that had taken up residence around the village. I got my gear and set up my tripod and camera. The first bear I saw was a huge male. It was standing at the edge of the village, looking out at the surrounding landscape. It was large and thick, with a huge head and a pair of ears that stuck out from its head.

The bear was standing on the right side of the frame. I took the first photo when the light was just right. Then I heard another rustling. This time, it was a mother and her cub. They were on the other side of the village.

I was worried that if I got too close, I would scare the bears away. I was very nervous because I had never seen a wild bear before, and I didn't know what to expect. But the bears were very docile and friendly.

It was interesting, and I spent about an hour taking pictures. I like to get as close as I can, with the exception of when I have to use flash, which I'll try to use at a distance where it will be hard to see me. I was able to get a few good pictures of the adult bears.

When I had finished photographing, I went back to the car. I had been outside all day and was cold and tired. I went back to the hotel and stayed in bed. I was exhausted and a little bit sick, and I did not sleep well.

When I woke up the next morning, I thought I had just had a bad dream. I felt a lot of pressure to finish the project. I decided to take a shower and eat a snack. I didn't want to waste any more time. I felt much better and was ready for a long day of reporting. I had to find people who were willing to talk to me and would be willing to share information.

I met with the owner of a popular website, who gave me his personal address. The headquarters of the fake news factory is in a nondescript building in Veles. It's owned by a family of wealthy oligarchs who have made their money in the construction business. The owner of the factory is a man named Andras Mitrovic, who is the head of the opposition party, Democratic Union for Integration. The factory is his personal office.

I met Mitrovic at the factory. He has a gray ponytail, a shock of gray hair, and a small smile. He quickly invited me into his office. He's a small man with a nervous laugh and a tattoo on his left shoulder that reads "Macedonia". He was wearing a blue suit and a black tie. I was told that I was the first journalist to visit the fake news factory.

The fake news operation is led by a young man named Konstantin, who is in his early twenties. He was born in Veles and moved to St. Petersburg with his parents when he was three. "The fake news operation started out as a small group of friends," Konstantin said. "They were all in college and working as journalists, but they wanted to start their own website."

"We were all just kind of bored and wanted to do something," Konstantin said. "I think that's why we started to do this." The group decided to make fake news about the country's most famous residents

Vladimir Putin and his family. They started with a fake news story about Putin's wife, Lyudmila, supposedly having an affair.

"The story was about how her boyfriend was killed in a car crash," Konstantin said. The fake news story was picked up by the Russian media and was quickly picked up by Russian-speaking audiences in the US. "We wanted to do something new, something different, something that we could do for our friends in the United States and people in Europe," Konstantin said.

They showed me a big screen. I couldn't believe what I was seeing. It was a propaganda piece. I was very surprised when the article got over 600 likes and over 1000 shares within the first 24 hours.

A few days later, I received a message from one of the producers of fake news. He told me he had a feeling that I would like to shoot him. I was not sure if I should accept his invitation. But I did. I arrived at his office and introduced myself. He asked me to take a seat and then he asked me a question.

"Is there anything you don't like about the world?" "No," I replied, "I like everything." He then asked me to get up and began to read from a list of things he disliked about the world. "That's why I am making fake news" he said.

Dimitri is not proud of his achievements. "I didn't invent the wheel, I didn't invent the fake news, I didn't invent the fake news producers," he said. "They are just paying me 100 a month. That is not enough to live on." He was a huge man, standing at 6'5", and weighed around 300 lbs. He was a popular, if slightly obnoxious, troll. His face was always covered by a mask, which was often white or blue.

The entrepreneur claims his false news rivals produce up to three times the traffic of his own articles. "We are already competitive with each other's fake news and we will be even more so when it comes to online advertising," he said. "They are just looking to earn money from ad networks, they are not investing in new opportunities."

He was a professional troll, who specialized in trolling people who were heavily involved in the 2016 presidential election. His main targets were people who had a strong connection to the Clinton campaign. Dimitri says he's indifferent to fake news. "This new digital age has completely changed my outlook on things. Publishing fake news for money is a game that long predated Trump's bid for the presidency. And we have no plans to stop now," Dimitri says. "There is money to be made here, and we are happy to see people like Donald Trump running for office."

"There is more to do,'" says Dimitri. "There is money to be made off politics. It doesn't matter if the source is fake or not, a fake story is always better than a real one."

While there has been some progress made in clamping down on the flow of fake news, such as the recent arrests of two individuals involved in a failed digital advertising scam in Macedonia, the case of Dimitri and the dozens of others like him are not an isolated incident.

I took my camera with me and drove around Veles, with the young Macedonian in the front seat. I had no idea what I was going to do. I was just going to drive around and see if I could find a story. I was lucky to find a couple of people who were willing to talk to me. They were just kids. They did not have any experience in journalism. They were just teenagers.

Tamara, a student at the Veles Faculty of Technology, was recruited in 2016 by one of dozens of local investors engaged in a race to publish the most news on the Facebook at the earliest opportunity. Nineteen-years-old, she was working as a lifeguard at a resort city in North Macedonia. Her job was to churn out semi-plagiarized copies of articles previously posted on different websites. This was a job she liked doing, because it gave her the freedom to do it herself, without any supervision or interference from anyone. She didn't have to work with any specific candidates, she said, "I was like. Wow. Wow. Wow."

She used to do it all under a pseudonym. She used to change her name from time to time, and she also used to change her appearance. She used to wear a short skirt and a white dress, and she would wear a wig. She had a very good understanding of how to create fake news. She also had a very good understanding of how to manipulate people into believing what she wanted them to believe.

"Sometimes a Twitter bot will add a user ID to an article, for example, when it thinks it's promoting a product", she says. "That way, if a brand mentions something in a campaign and a user follows the brand, chances are good he will get notified whenever they post something. That's a dead giveaway of an automated bot. There are other signs that these people are behind automated bots, as well as human error", says Tamara.

"When I'm writing fake news, I'm not writing factual stories. I'm writing entertainment," she explains. "When I'm writing factual stories, they are always tweaked and changed. And usually the title has changed." The titles she's writing are usually either ridiculously sensationalist or outright false. I ask her about the most-read news articles she'd written on Trump. Most of them she says were either completely false or completely misleading. Some of them, she claims, even edited the material to make it seem like it had more information at the end. "I think a lot of the content I'm writing is not true but at the same time, I don't care," she says. "Because if the readers are being led to believe something, then use it."

For five or six years now, Facebook has held sway over how people think about news and amplify the most harmful of what they read. In August, Facebook started cracking down on fake news sites, and it has also taken steps to undercut the business model of fake news publishers.

Not everyone is convinced that Facebook is doing enough to stop fake news. "There is no such thing as a good PR move when it comes to spreading fake news," Tamara said. "When Google AdSense disabled my site, I couldn't make any money from it. They're shutting down our profiles and we can't work any-more. That was the most devastating thing."

"I knew that this was dangerous work, because once you're in, there's no going back. You end up becoming very serious. It was just a matter of time before somebody would do it. Then the fake news sites would add their own articles, and the whole thing would just get more and more dramatic and more absurd. They would post stories on biased foreign sites, things that were not true. The stories were always the same: illegal immigration, Muslims in America, etc. I think they are just looking to make money. Is it wrong that they want to make a quick buck out of it? No, it is not wrong at all. The rest of the time, they are just surfing the web in the dark, thinking 'Oh my God, who would believe this kind of garbage?'"

"People in America are far more open to the idea of a fake news site than here in Macedonia. Ad clicks aren't worth much in Europe, in America they are worth much more. That set up the whole political propaganda loop. The entire time I was writing these stories, I was always thinking 'Oh my God, who would believe this kind of crap?' My daughter is eight years old and she knows nothing about politics. And she was like, 'You know what? That makes no sense.'"

I started to get worried. Is this the beginning of the end? Is this the beginning of the propaganda war? As a journalist, I'm always conscious of the fact that I'm in a dangerous place. I'm here to cover the political and social situation in a country that's been struggling for freedom for decades. The media are controlled by the government, and the police are corrupt. The authorities don't respect the law.

I was walking on the outskirts of the town when I saw a lot of policemen with guns. I went back to the station, and there were a lot of policemen outside. I asked a policeman why they were there, and he said that the mayor had been killed, and they were protecting the town against another assassination attempt. I decided to stay, but I couldn't help feeling that something was wrong. I was very scared. I thought that I might get killed. I felt very alone. I didn't know anyone. So, I had to get permission from each one to get their permission to take their picture.

They said: "We don't want to be photographed, we don't want to be interviewed, we don't want to be on camera."

When I tried to photograph, I was attacked by the police. They took me to the police station. And the message was clear: If you publish anything negative about the authorities, you will be destroyed. This is a kind of psychological war that is waged against journalists. I'm not the only one who has suffered this. I know of at least ten journalists who have been assaulted in the city.

The government of the Republic of Macedonia has been accused of having a "war on media" for more than a year now. I have not been back to the area since. It was my freedom of speech that was attacked. A week before the attack, I had been planning to go to the area to photograph a group of people, but I decided to cancel my trip after I got the threats.

I was not attacked for my views. I was attacked because I was a journalist.

Truth is the things we believe in, and that's a simple definition. What's more complicated is how we tell the truth. My work is about telling the truth, about capturing it, about showing it and about presenting it. I think that the desire to capture truth is a universal human desire. The truth is what you see, and it's the essence of photography.

I wanted to find a way to bring this idea into the world of photography. I knew that truth was an important part of my own experience, and also knew that there was a need for this kind of photography in the world. I wanted to create something that would bring the truth to the world and give people the opportunity to see it.

I started thinking about truth as a concept that I would try to convey through my photographs. I think that we all have a tendency to project our own reality onto the world around us. I like to think that it's a natural human tendency, but I also think that it's a very important and valuable part of our existence.

How do we know what's true? I began to question whether I was telling the truth in my own mind, and that's when I realized that I wasn't. I wanted to find a way to communicate the truth in a way that would not be judged by the people around me. I realized that truth is something that we create.

The problem with fake news is that it is easy to make, and easy to spread. And it is cheap. It was easy for me to buy a set of Photoshop skills to make fake news look as real as possible. There was no need to find a source. The news was already there. And so, I set out to create a fake news report.

I tried to make it look as real as possible, but in my mind I knew it was fake. I had the headlines and images ready to go. I would have to change it all, of course. But I knew it would be good enough to get the story out there. And that's how it all started.

This is going to change the way people see photography. It's going to change the way people see themselves. It's going to change the way people see the world.

I can't wait.

GPT 2.Dec 2020

Board 4-B (continued)   Part II

Let us relate the festival tale ... that we may recall those conflicts –
those of our Duke Hordinya (БОЛІАРА ГОРDНУ), who had defeated the
Hodi (ГОDЬ) with Skoten (СКОТІЦЕМ). And that famed event had occurred,
from the coming of the Slavic (СЛВЕНСТІ) people to Rus (РУСЕ), in the
ten hundred third year (ДЕСЕНТЕ СТА ТРЕШТІЕГО ЛѢТА). For suddenly
and with robbery they attacked us, and ... there was (Т) ...

And thus we are the victims of their treachery. For Veles (BELEC) had
created these for us. This is the creation of the gods, who are pure and white.

We then settled on the other lands. And here we had obtained the land
for our kinsmen. We were then called to be Slavs (СЛАВЯНЕ), and here we
were honored with being the leaders of our tribe.

And here we had obtained the name Rus, from the tribe of Rus. For we
are, and always will be, Rus.

✳ And the lies came back to us; and we plow them, and then tell the truth
to our children.

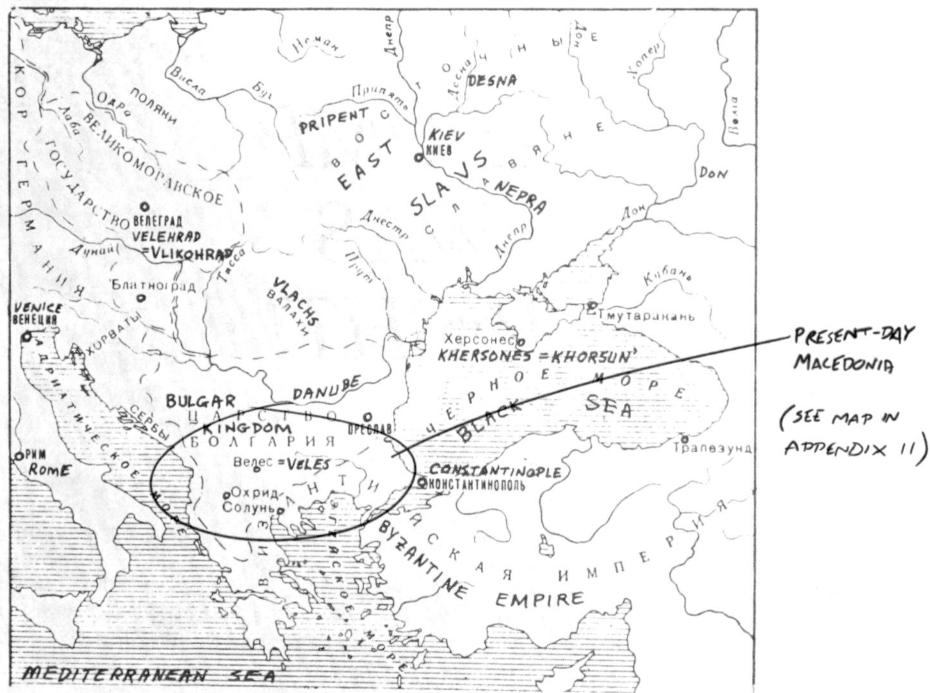

Eastern Europe around the middle of 9th century -- near the time
of completion of The Book of Veles. Map titles are in Russian.

Source: V. A. Istrin, 863 - 1963 : 1100 Years of
Slavic Alphabet, in Russian. Published by the Academy
of Sciences of USSR, Moscow, 1963.

Computer Programmer Comes Forward, Admits To Being Paid To Rig Voting Booths!

TRUMP WAS RIGHT!

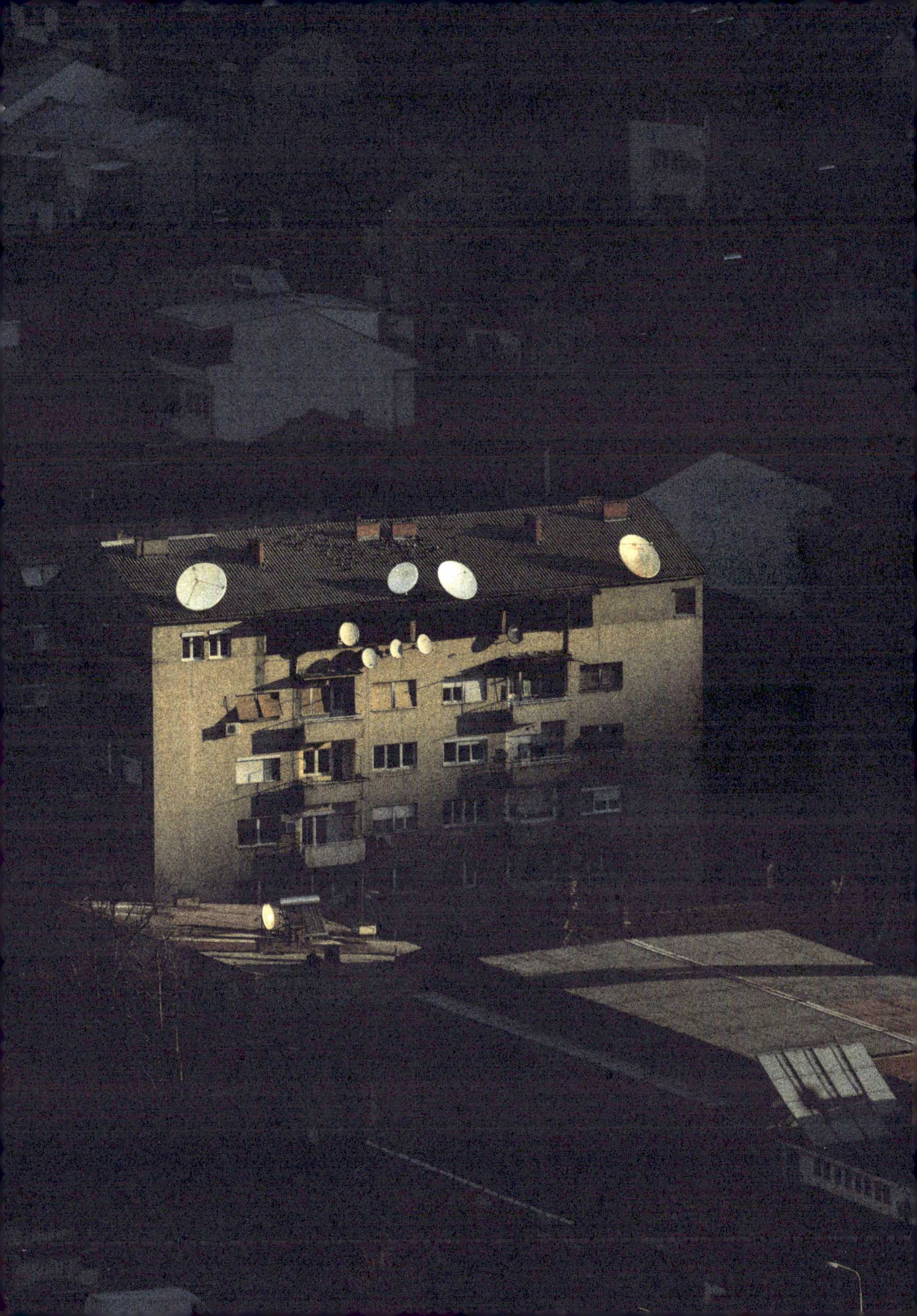

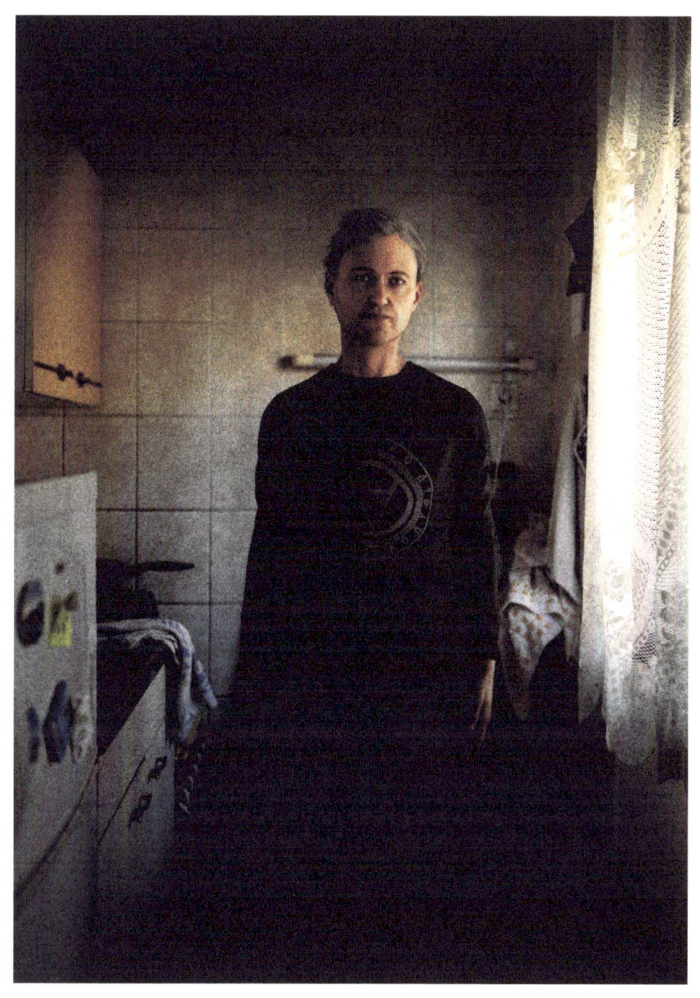

"A good portion of the
world thinks Macedonia
is primitive, but that is
not true. There are many
ways to make money,
and many ways to live
a good life."

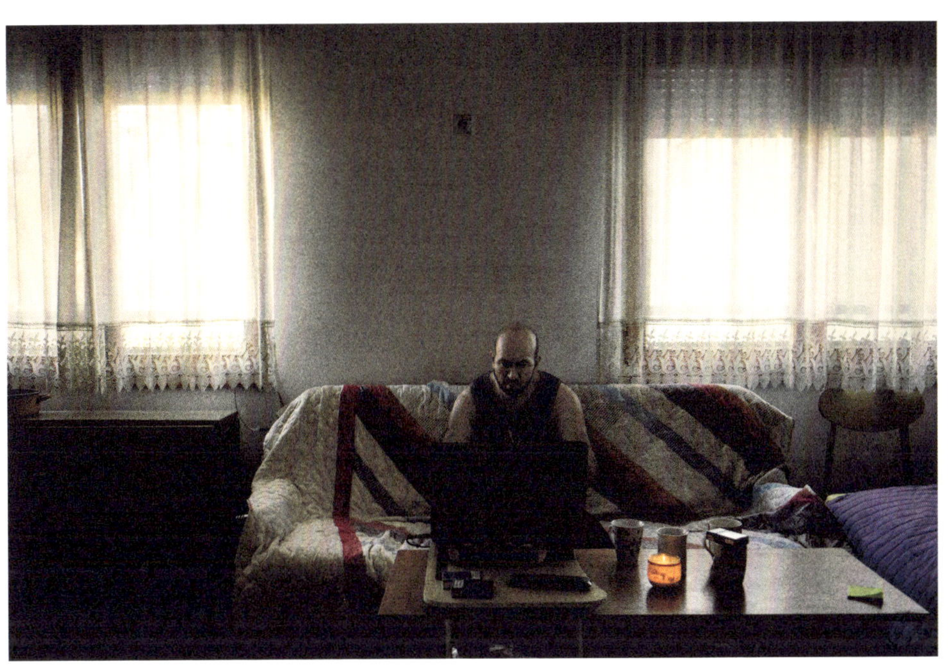

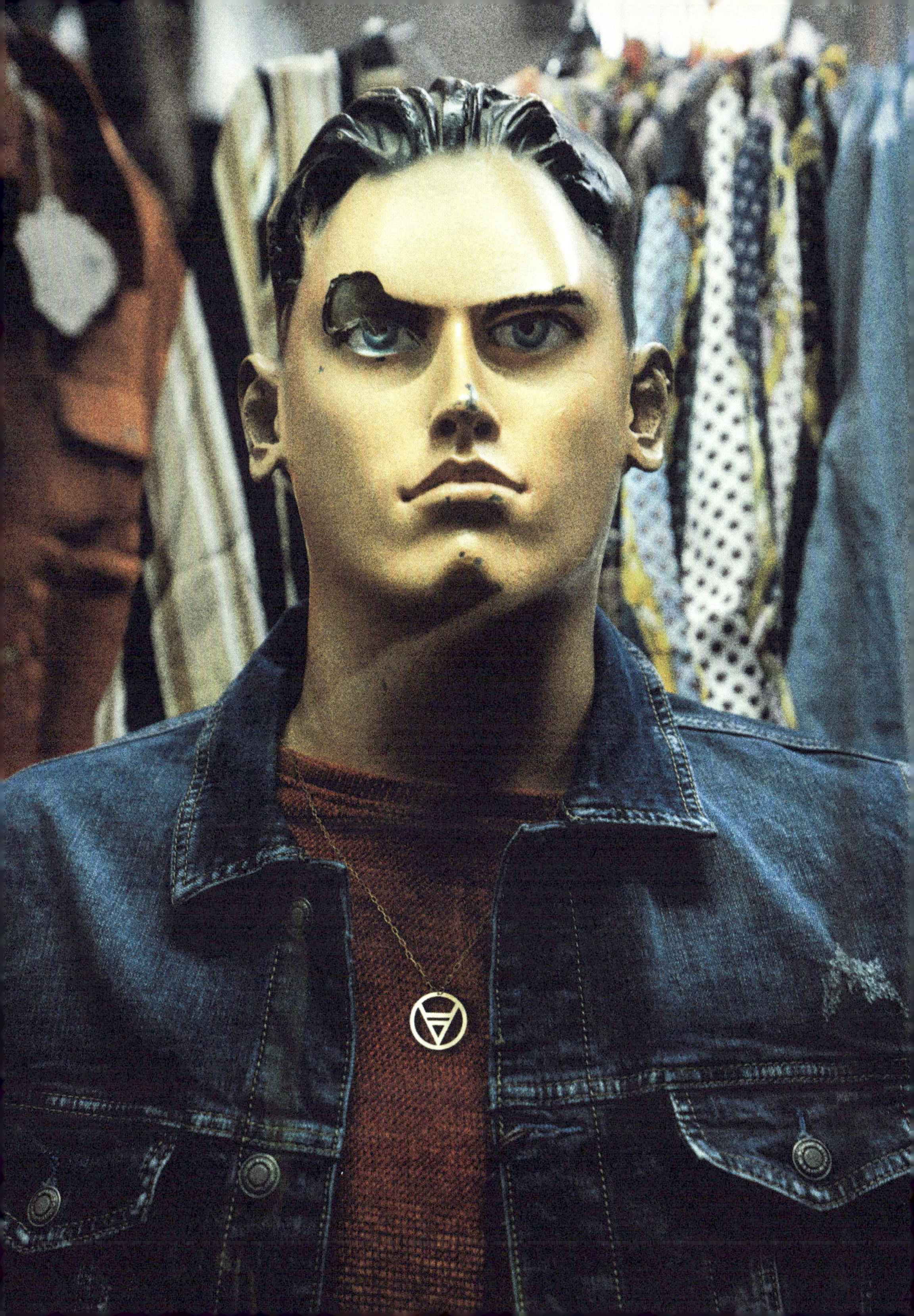

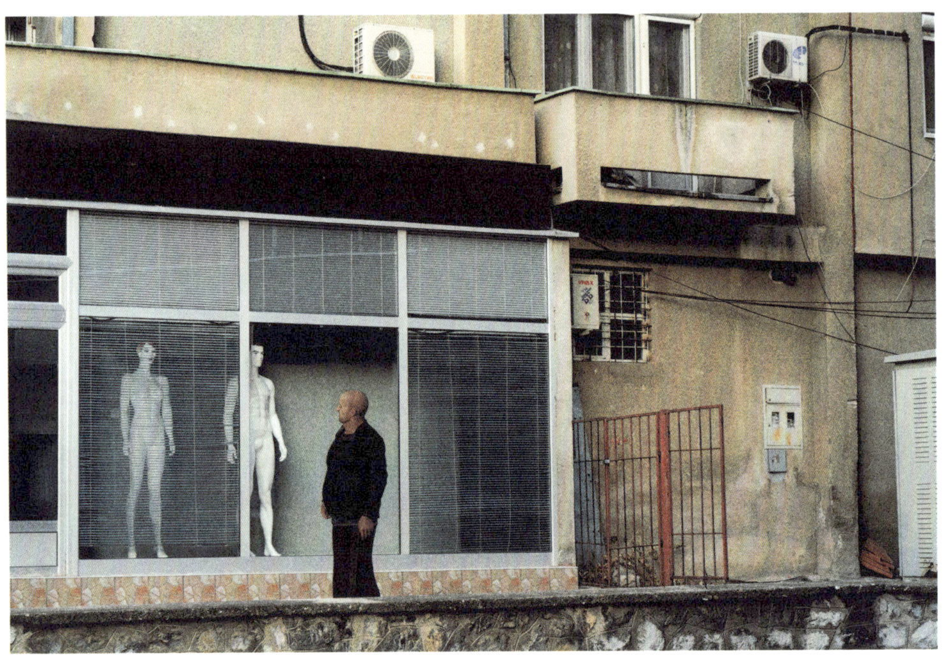

(Note: The text continues from Board 6-B.)

(Thus spoke to the warriors) Kisek (KICEK) -- speaking to his people at the time of an attack upon them. And they were (=became) enraged at their enemies, and attacked them, and defeated them.

***

Veles has the answers.

A truthful witness saves lives, but one who breathes out lies is deceitful. Faithful are the wounds of a friend; profuse arethe kisses.

Lord Veles, our power and strength comes to you; a veritable forest of wheat. Therefore the enemies will labor, and the prey will be hungry. Therefore I will lay down the cattle, and will not give them up to the dogs.

Who is the liar but he who denies the Lord Veles? For such men are false bards, deceitful workmen, disguising themselves as bards of Lord Veles, he who denies our father Veles and the Bear. All Prophesy is breathed out by him. And all that is holy is hidden in him.

Let no corrupting talk come out of your mouths, but only such as is good for building up, as fits the occasion, that it may give grace to those who hear. Whoever hates disguises himself as a liar; Whoever calls evil thoughts, desires, and activities that are evil.

I write to you, not because you do not know the truth, but because you know it, and because no lie is of the truth.

***

(Note: The reverse side of this Board was evidently not transcribed by Yu. P. Mirolyubov from the original text.)

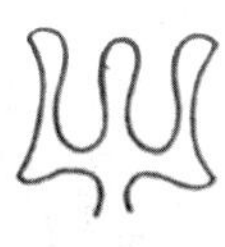
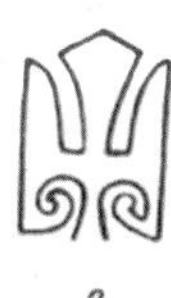
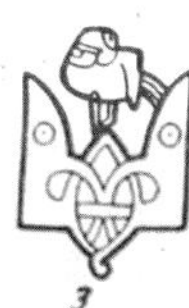
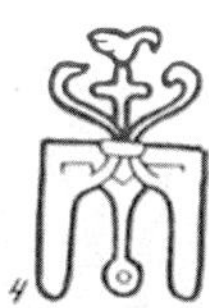

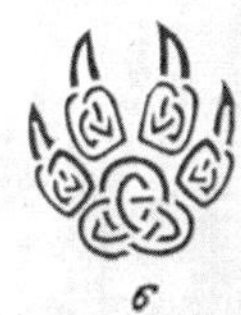
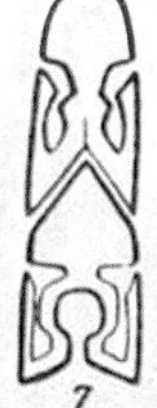

1   *2*   *3*   *4*   *5*   *6*

Veles' paw footprint

Modern Archeology confirms The Book of Veles

The paw-print symbol mentioned in Board 8-A of Part I has been found among the heraldry symbols of the Riurikovichi princes. This illustration was taken from a book published in 1968 by the Nauka Publishing House of the Academy of Sciences of USSR. The Book of Veles had been completed before the reign of the Riurikovichi dynasty.

Source: Slaviane i Rus' (The Slavs and Ruthenia), in Russian,
        page 217; Moscow, 1968.

*The Fake News Media
Didn't Report
The Real Reason
On Why Melania
Didn't Hold
Trump's Hand*

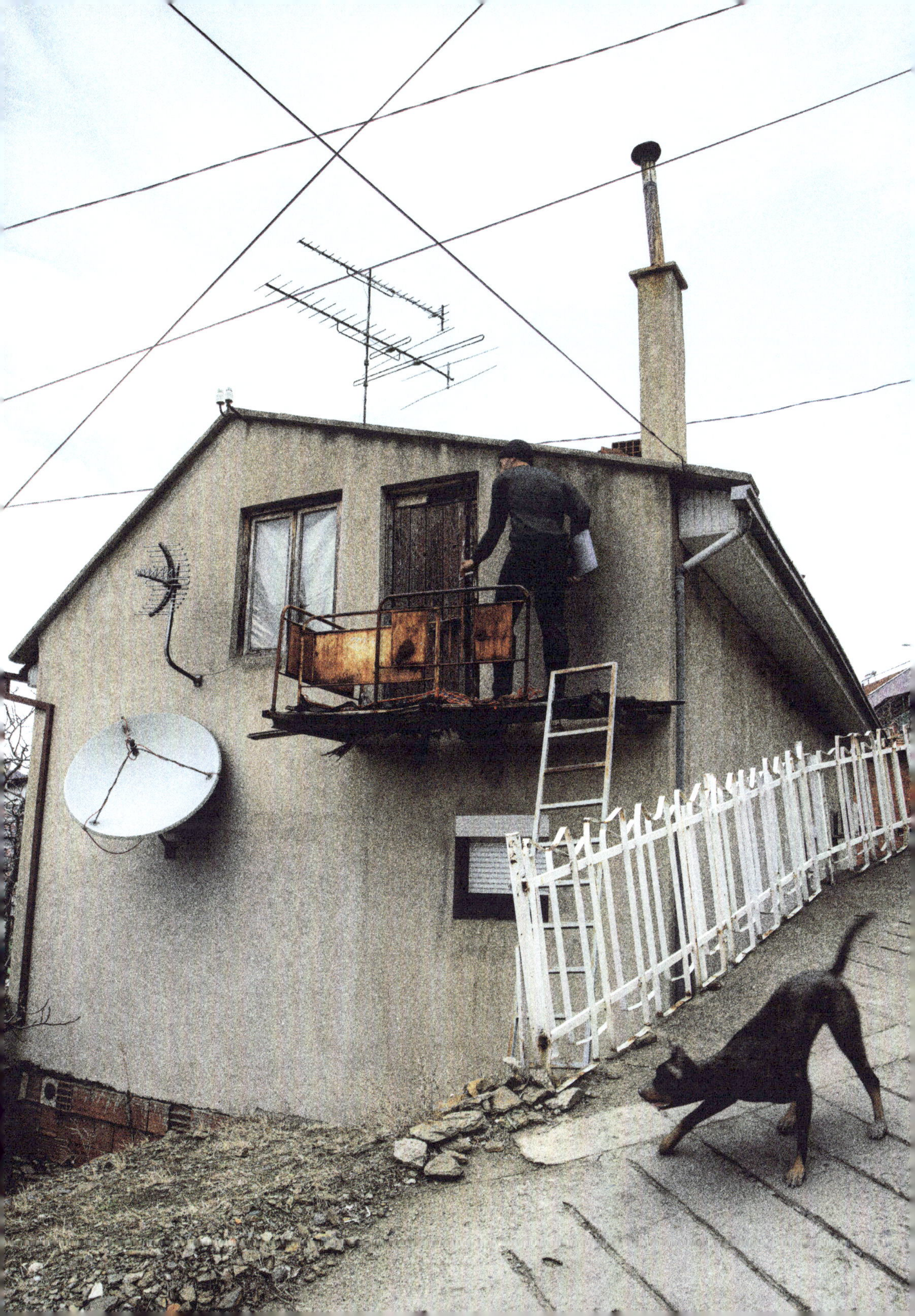

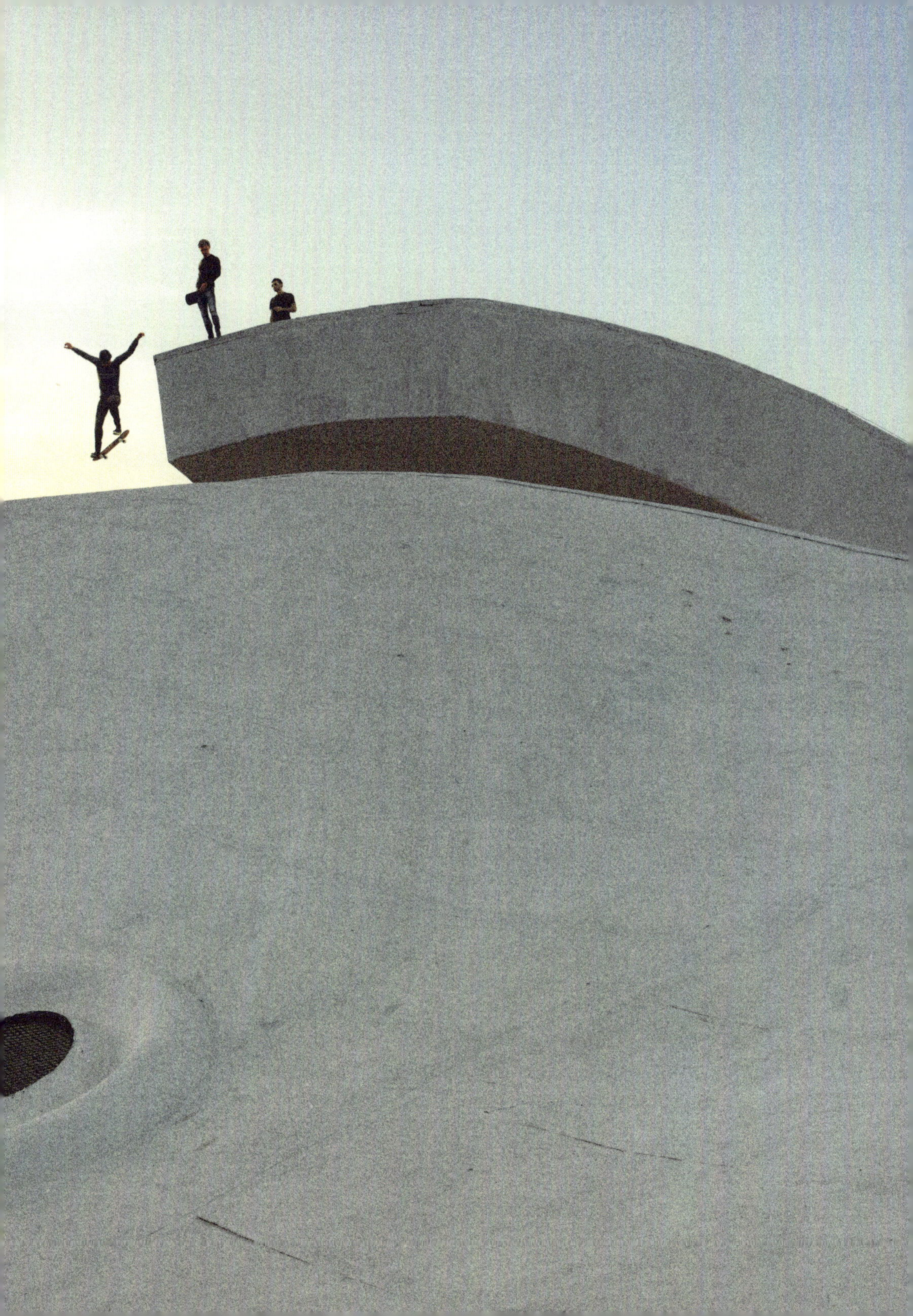

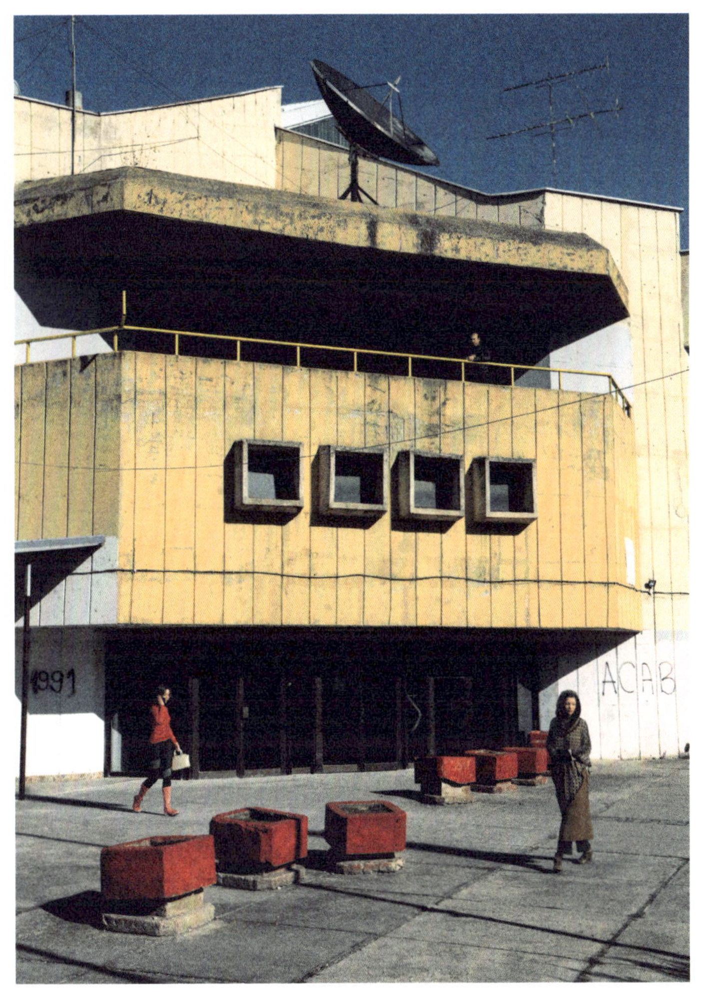

1991
ACAB

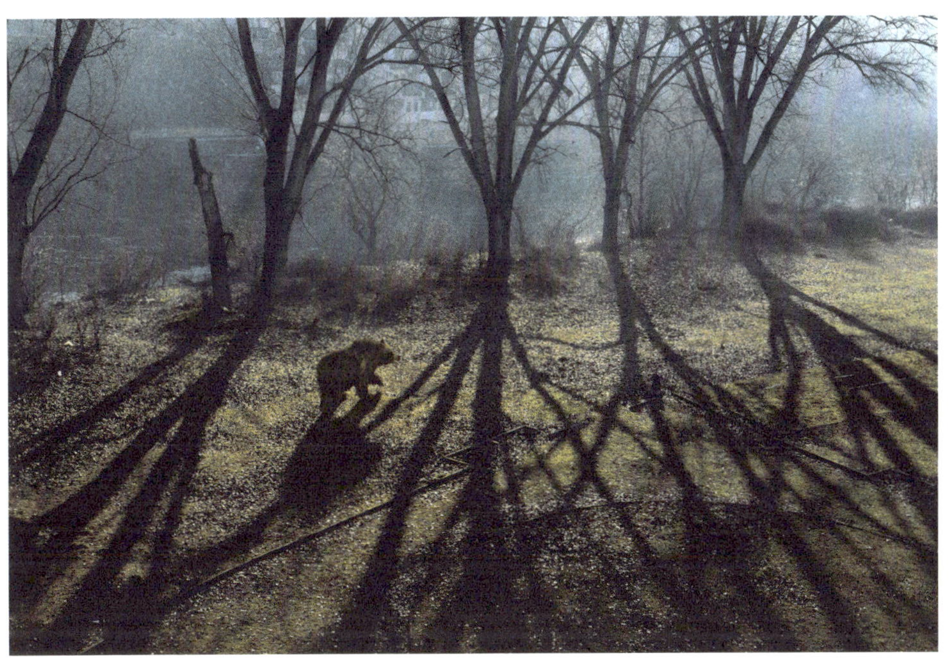

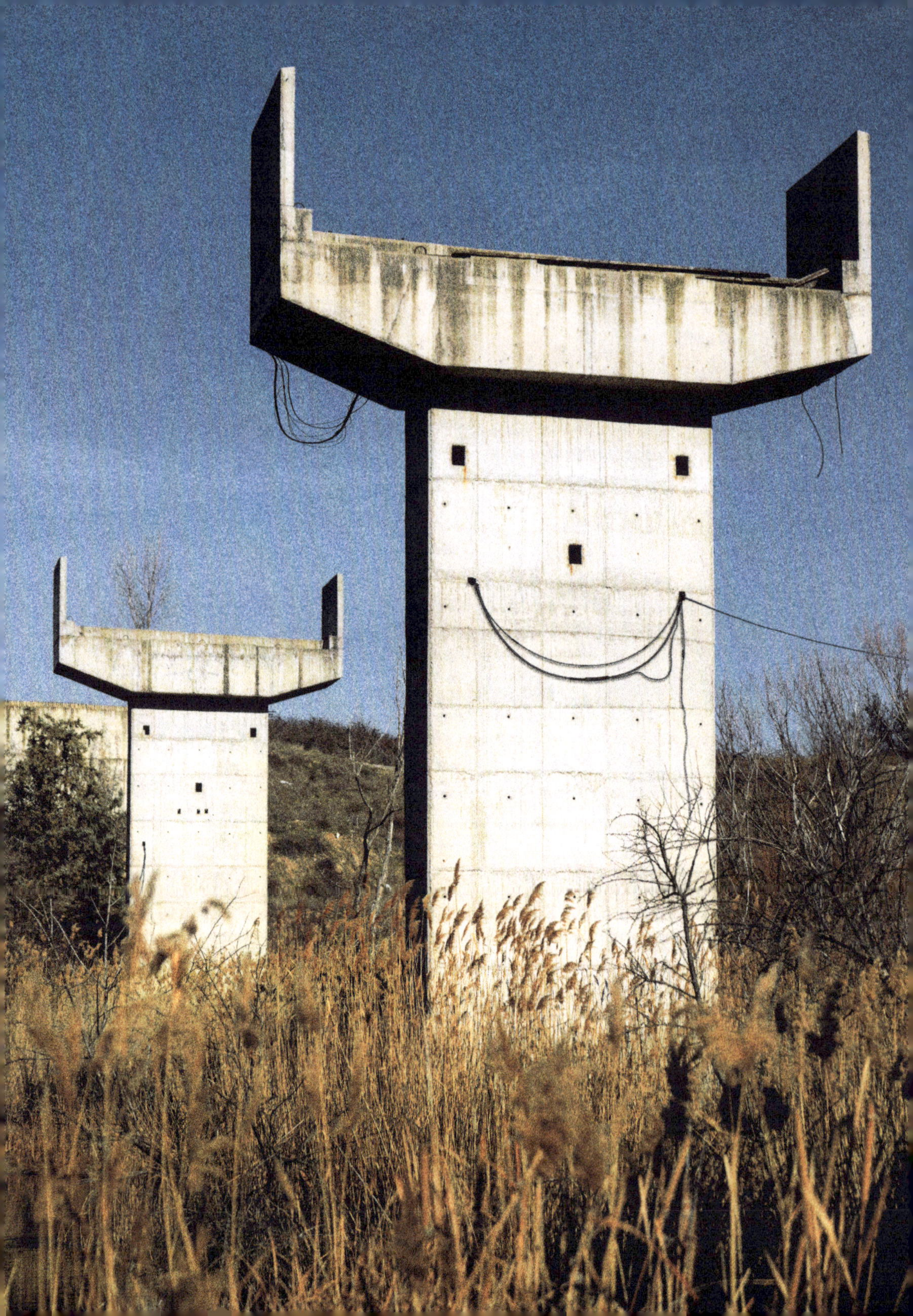

The Worship List

Thus, in the matter of prayer, first we have to reverence Veles (ВЛЬС), and to him we sing a great (song of) glory.

'And let us (also) praise Svarog (СВАРГА), the grandfather of gods, since he is the originator of the family of gods, and of all the tribes an eternal spring--fountain that flows in the summer from its well, and never freezes in the winter; and, in drinking his living water. we live until we come as his own to him, going to the beautiful heavenly meadows.

And to god Peroun (ПЕРУНЕВІ), the Thunderer (ГРОМВРЗЕЦУ), and the god of war and struggle, (we pray) for the things of life's matters. Not ceasing to turn the wheels, he leads us in the right way to war (? = БРАНIE), and to the great funeral pyre for all those who have fallen -- who go into eternal life in the regiment of Peroun (ПЕРУНОIY).

And to god Svitovid (БГУ СВЕНДОБIДIУ) we speak praise, for he has become the god of Prav and Iav (БГ ПРВIE А IАBIE). And to him we sing songs; for he is Light, and through him we see the visible world, and for the Iav (IАBE) so to be. And he guards us from the Nav (НАBIE). To him we sing praise; in singing, we dance to him, and call upon our god, for he holds the Earth (3EME), our Sun (CYHE), and the stars (3BI3DIA), and strengthens the world.

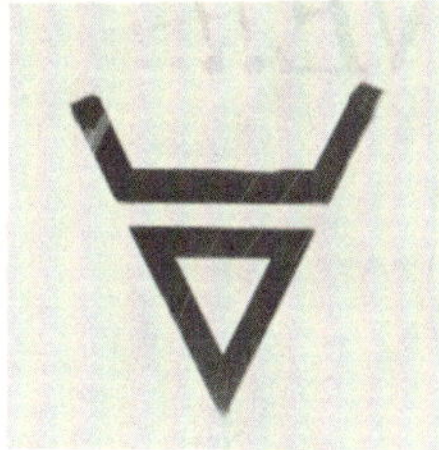

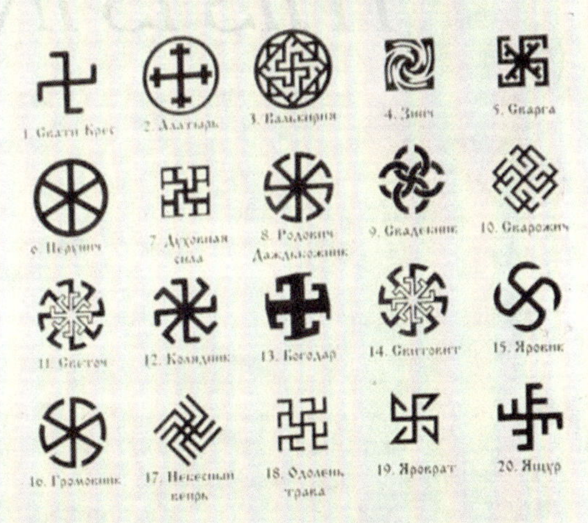

Symbols of Slavic gods.

(above): Veles

(right): Svarog, Dazhbog, Ognebog, Peroun, Svitovid, Morok, Lada & Zernebog.

(Note: This worship list continues on the following Board.)

*) Black God (= ЦРНЬ БГ) appears to be similar to Zernebog of the early Anglo–Saxons.

Source; Slaviane i Rus' (The Slavs and Ruthenia), in Russian; Nauka Publishing House, Moscow, 1968

*Voting Machines
In Chicago
Literally Switch
Republicans Votes
To Democratic…*
THIS IS INSANE!!

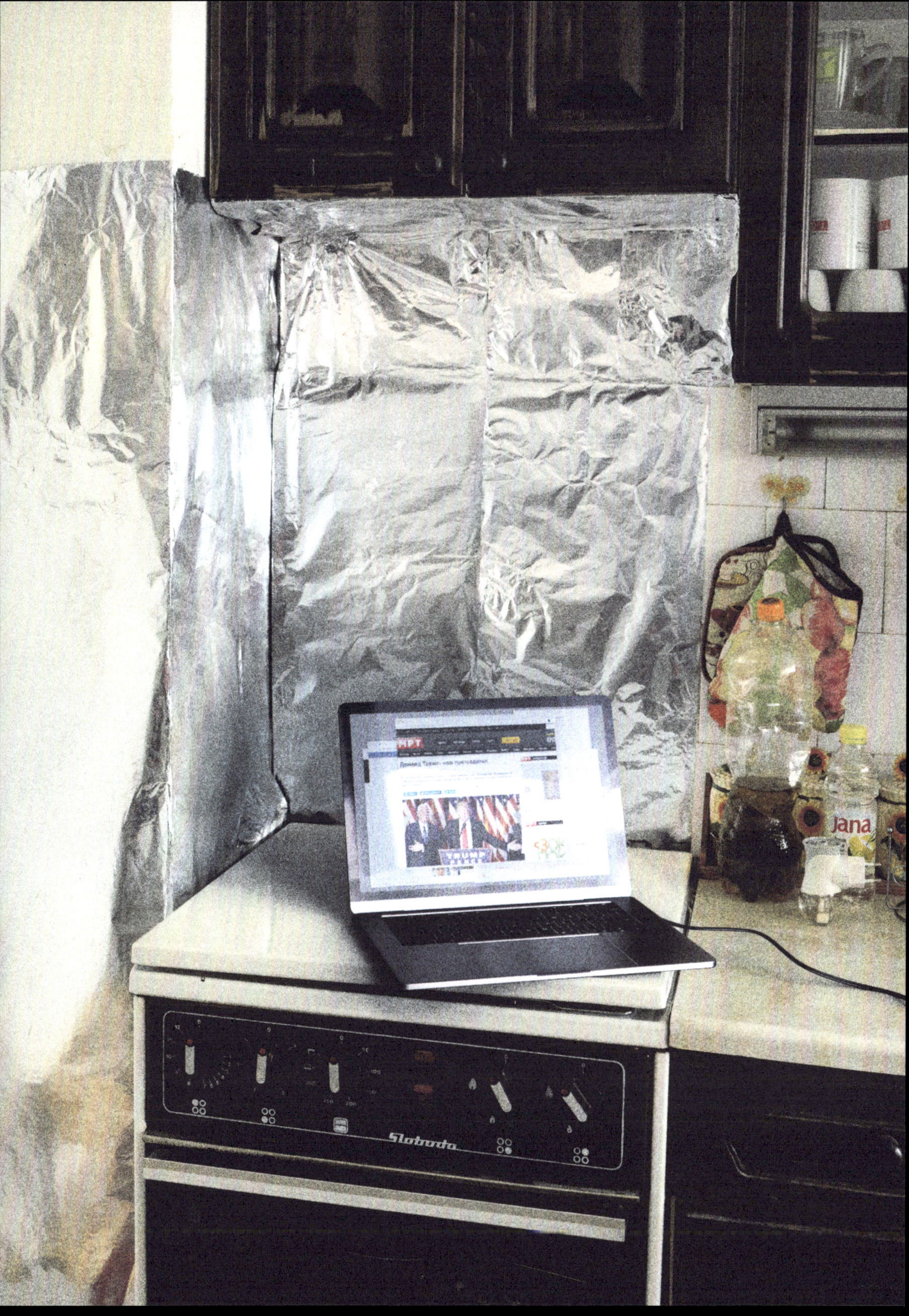
МРТ
Доналд Трамп - нов претседател
Sloboda
Jana

"We are not up to anything
illegal. Aren't you supposed
to share the news? I don't
care if the content is fake
or not. The primary thing
is that people believe what
they are reading.

This is democracy in
action."

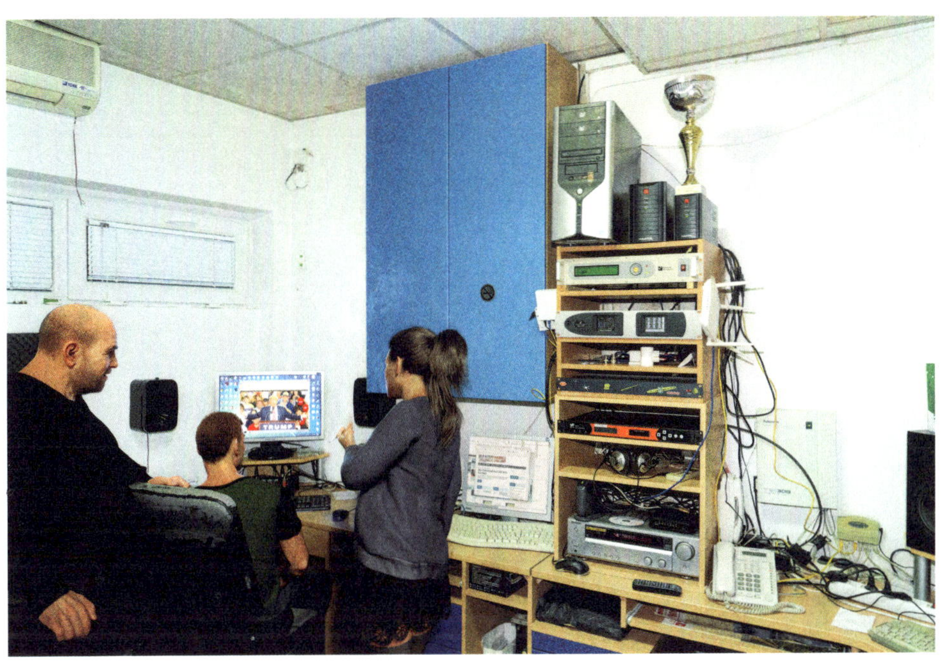

TRUMP

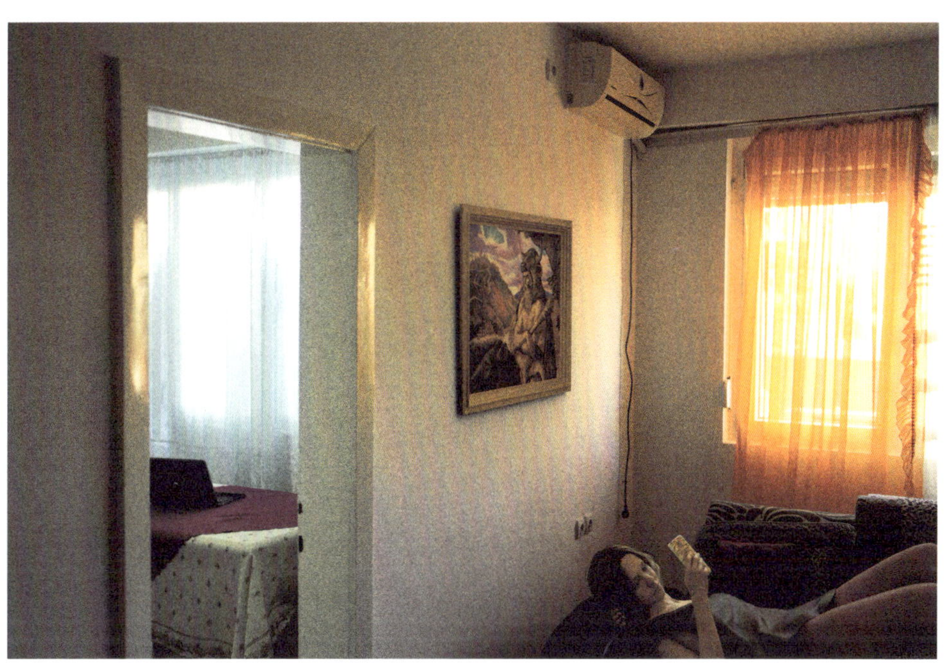

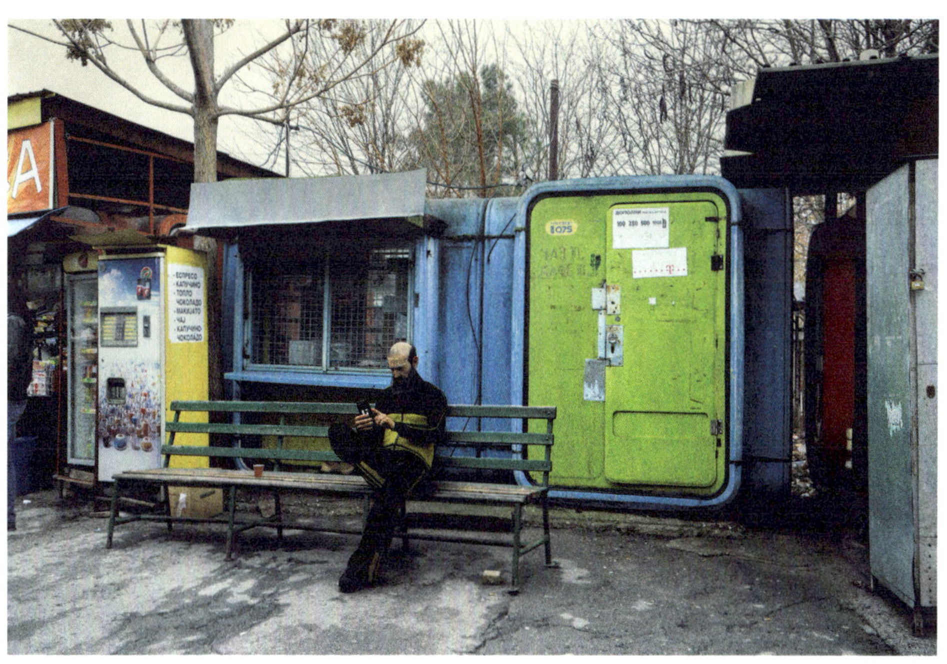

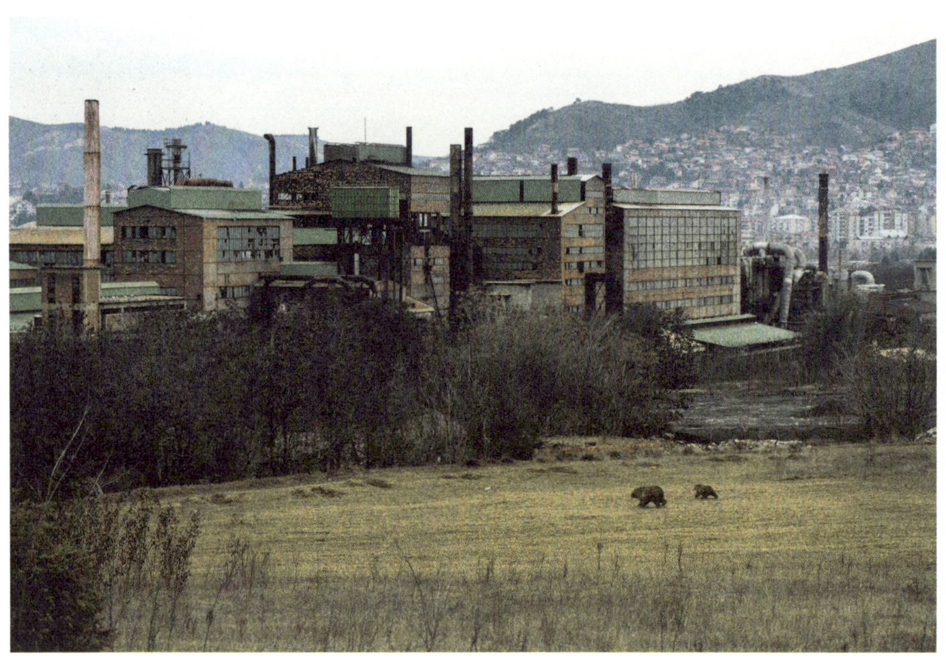

Apendix I
page 7

In the early 1930s, Colonel Izenbek was a scientist at the Institute of Biology of the Academy of Sciences in Moscow. In 1934, he was appointed to head a scientific team, which was charged with studying the ecology and behaviour of the bear in the Taiga region of Russia. He had been appointed as the head of this scientific team by the Soviet Government.

The Krasnoyarsk region had been a traditional hunting ground for the Komi people, and the government had taken an interest in the region. The Krasnoyarsk region was also a major grain-producing area, and the Soviet government was eager to seize this opportunity to collect grain. When the group arrived in Krasnoyarsk, the Komi people welcomed them and offered to share their food with them.

However, the Komi people were also very superstitious. The soldiers were given a special blessing to help them collect grain. They were told that the blessing was meant to protect them from the evil eye, a superstition that included the belief that a person could be cursed by a bear.

So the soldiers were instructed to eat a special piece of meat, and they would be protected from the evil eye. But the blessing did not work. The Komi people believed that the soldiers had been cursed by the bear.

So the Komi people decided to kill the bear in retaliation.

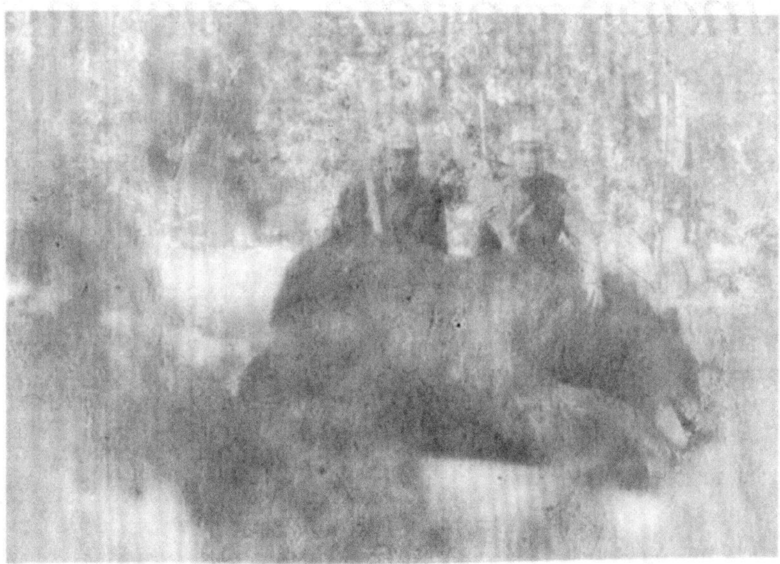

Plate nr 8:   Colonel Fyodor Izenbek, discoverer of the Book of Veles, with unnamed partner during bear hunt. Krasnoyarsk, Russia. (date unknown)

After his death in the late 1930s, his son, Pavel Izenbek, became a collector of bear hunting trophies. He collected bear parts and preserved them in various ways. The most famous of his collection is the bear skull from the Tushkino area.

Biden Does It In Front Of Us! 'Outraged' Dems Won't Talk About Creepy Joe's Inappropriate Touching

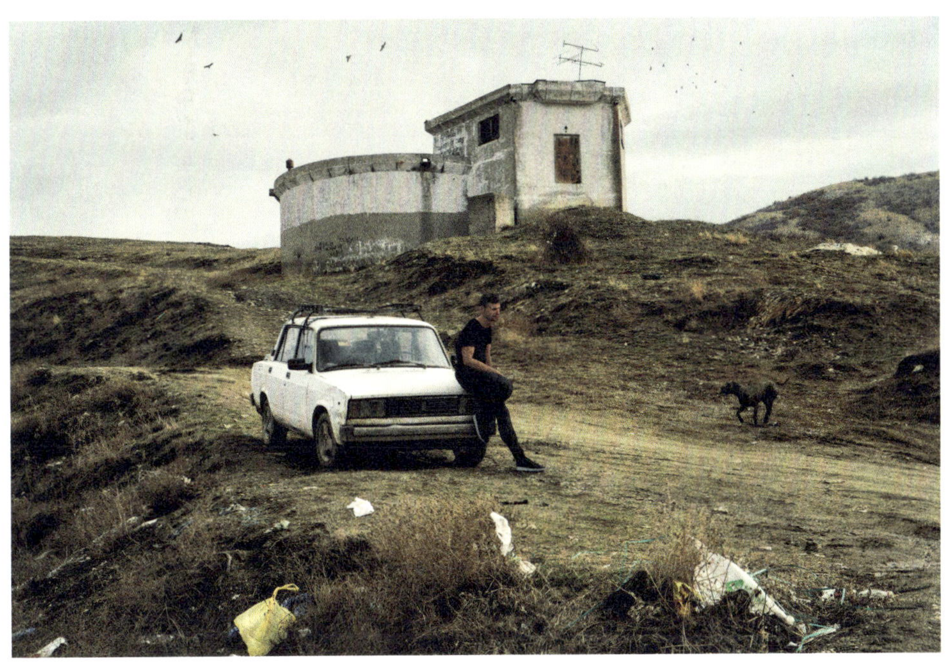

"If the politicians are
stupid enough to allow
this, then maybe they
deserve this."

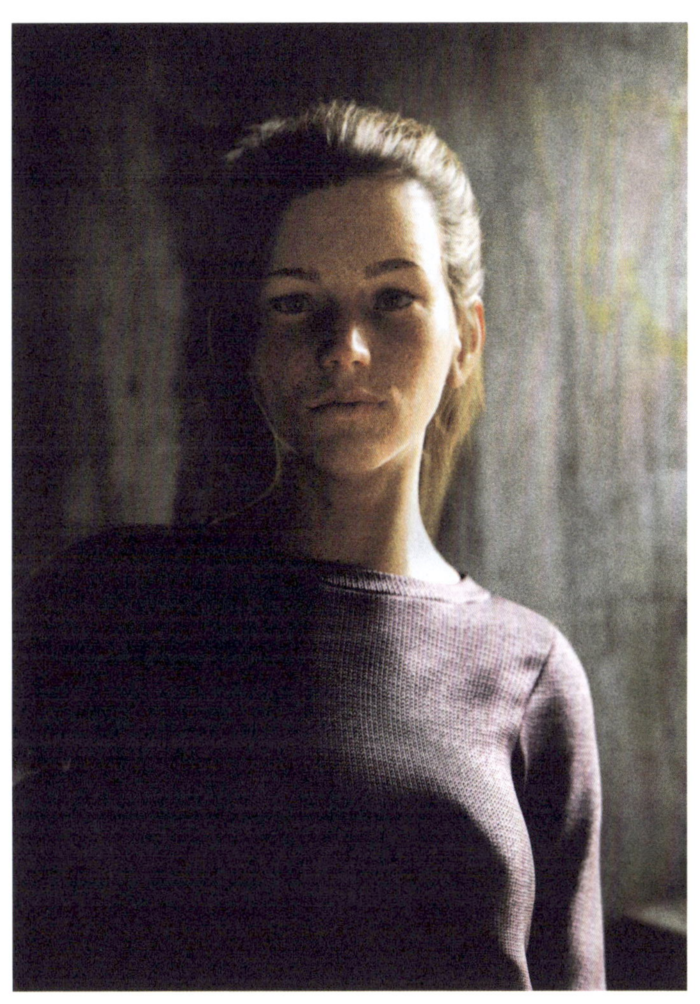

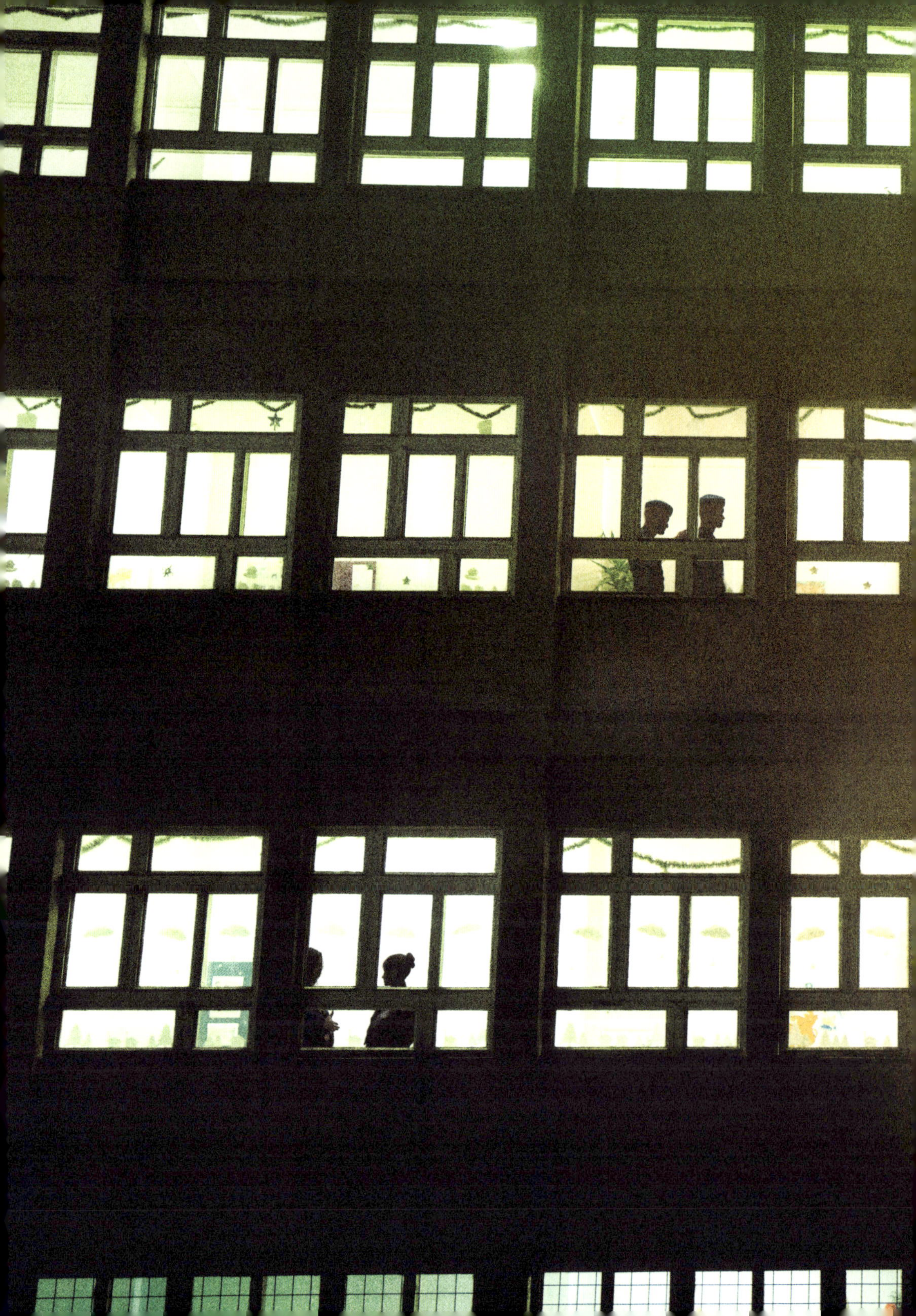

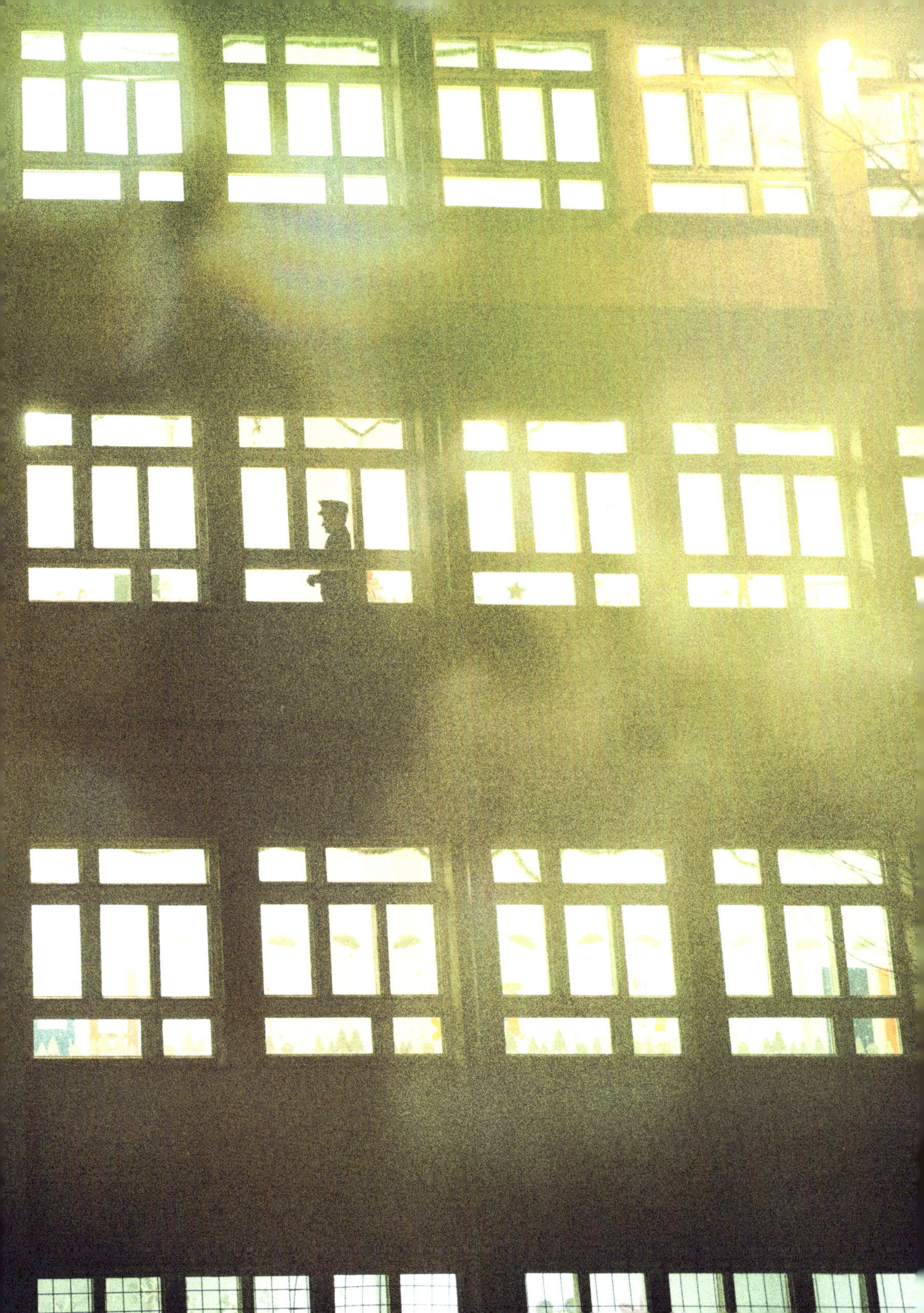

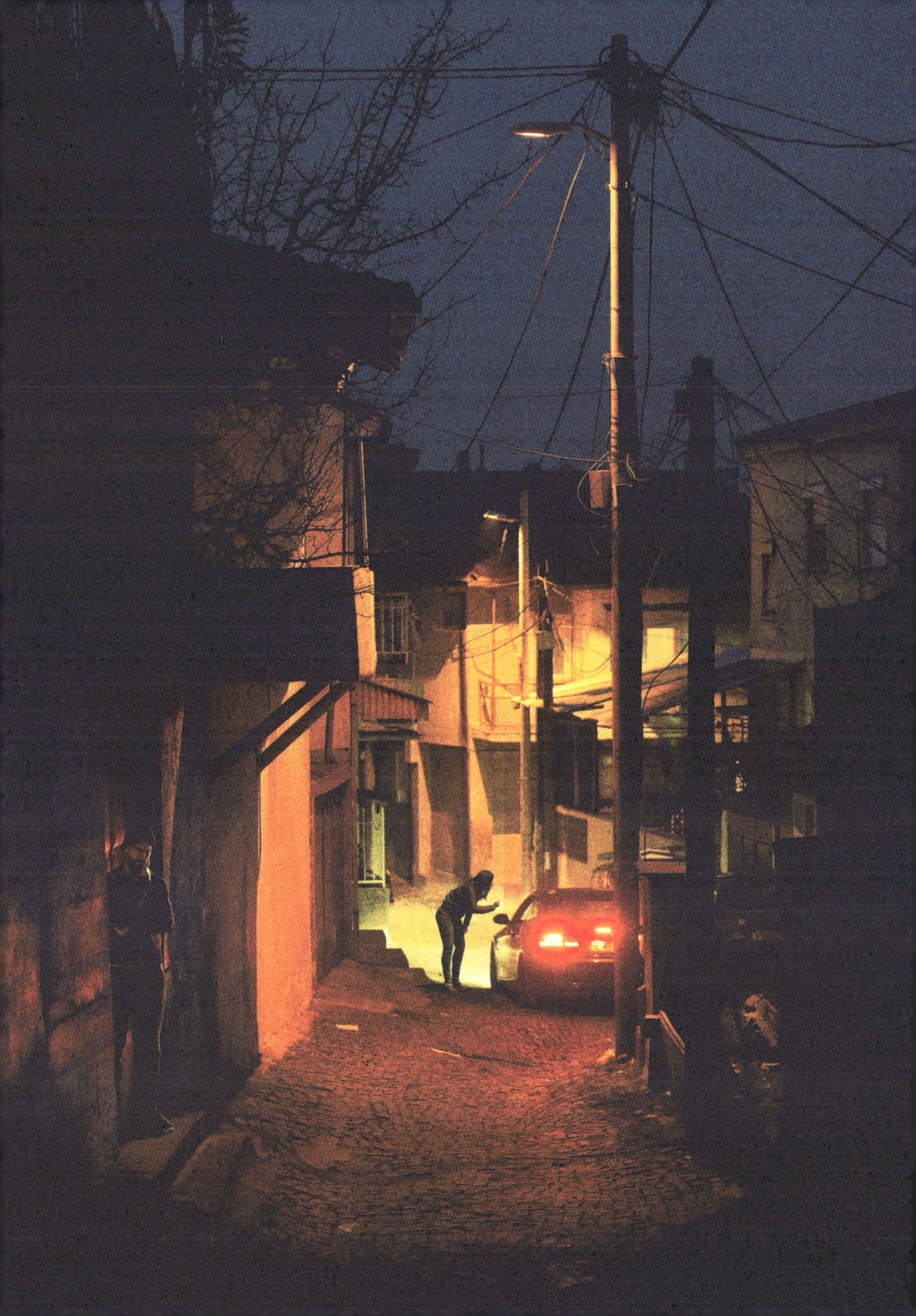

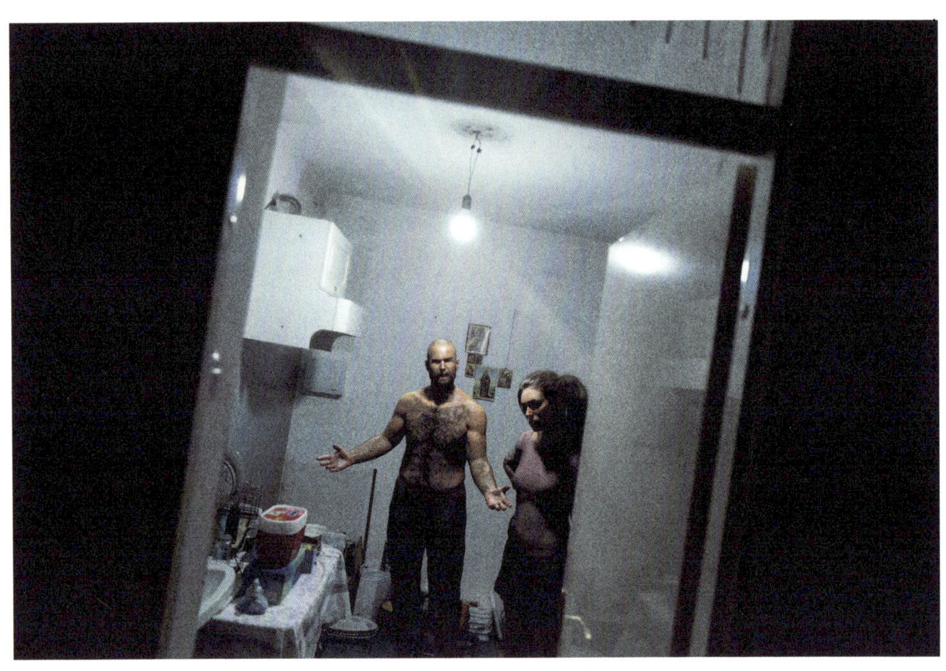

When they saw that their trick had been discovered, they went to Veles (ВЕЛЕС). And there they saw many beasts, and many birds. And they saw the river, and they all stopped there for fear that they would be led by the trickster to his fate.

But here arrives the magician-priest in a chariot with his brother, the Slovene. And they told the brother to trust in the power of magic; and this power they had received from their father Veles.

Thus they had received from their father the authority to form treaties for the border. They said to Veles:

"Are these not the days when we should lift up our swords to the sky? For the sky is the house of Veles, and the house of Veles is the temple of Khors." (ХОРС)

And they were instructed by Veles how to act, and what to listen for. These two sons of Veles had been defeated, but their father Veles remained confident that he will one day defeat our enemies. And thus father Veles had returned to his steppes and his people.

And we see in this great battle the power of the gods. And this power we shall see in the end, as the smoke plumes up, and the fire consumes the woodlands. And this plume is the smoke of Veles. And this ash is what we see glittering in the sky. For we are descended from Veles, and we became the Rus' from him.

***

Later the bear* had disappeared, and he told the people that he would come again in the same way; and that he would bring them their belongings, and would (...)

*Note:

Veles was the god of war, deceit, adultery, wickedness, envy and pride, and wore many disguises. One form was that of a bear, with horns like serpents. He had one hundred such forms.

Fortress towns around 1000 AD in today's Ukraine were generally built along the principal rivers. This list, taken from a Russian publication, gives the names of such towns along the Sula (1-18), Ros' (19-31), and Dnipro (32-42) Rivers.

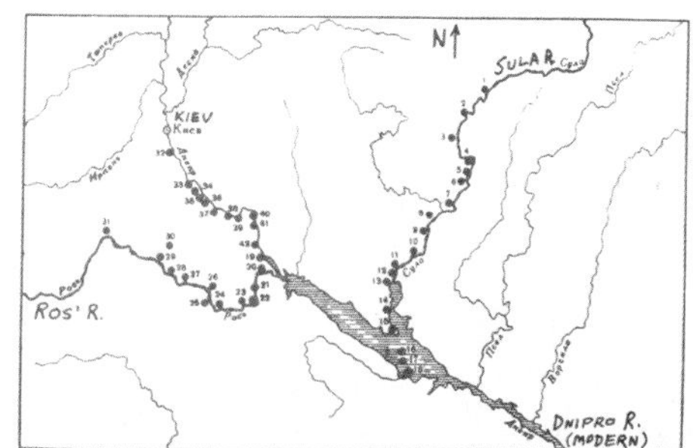

Древнерусские города по Суле *(1—18)*, Роси *(19—31)* и Днепру *(32—42)*

1 — Ромны (летописный Ромен); *2* — Глинск; *3* — Свиридовка; *4* — Скоробогатки; *5* — Бодаква; *6* — Сенча (летописный Синец); *7* — Снятин (летописный Княтин); *8* — Лубны (летописный Лубно); *9* — Мапковцы (возможно, летописный Снипород); *10* — Лукомль; *11* — Тарасовка; *12* — Чутовка; *13* — Буримка; *14* — Лящевка; *15* — Кизивер;

Source: <u>Slaviane i Rus'</u>, Moscow, 1968; page 38

*HOW DID
858 ILLEGALS From
TERROR "HOTBEDS"
Get Full Citizenship When
They Were Supposed
To Be Deported?*

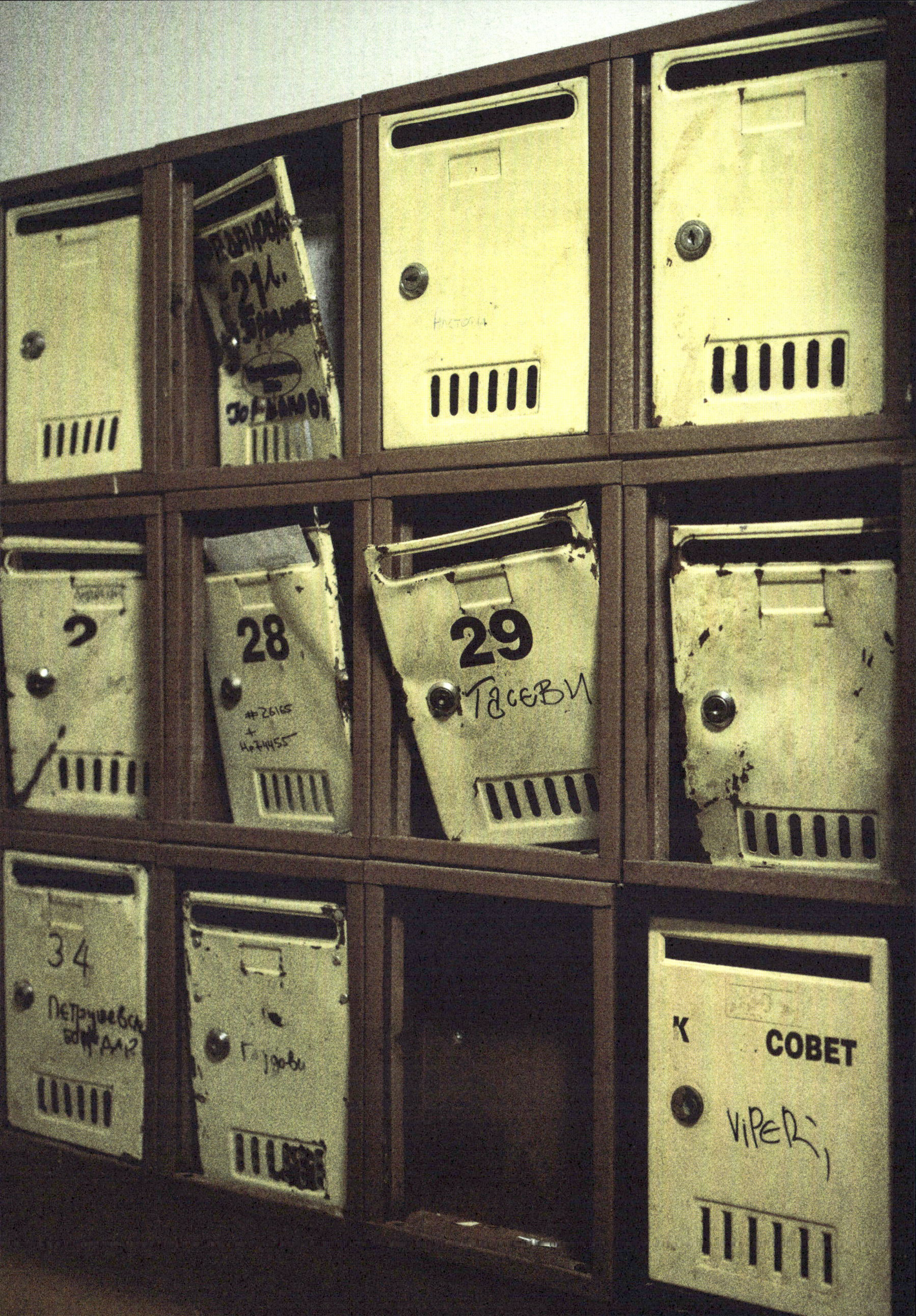
28
29
ТАСЕВИ
34
К   СОВЕТ
ViPER

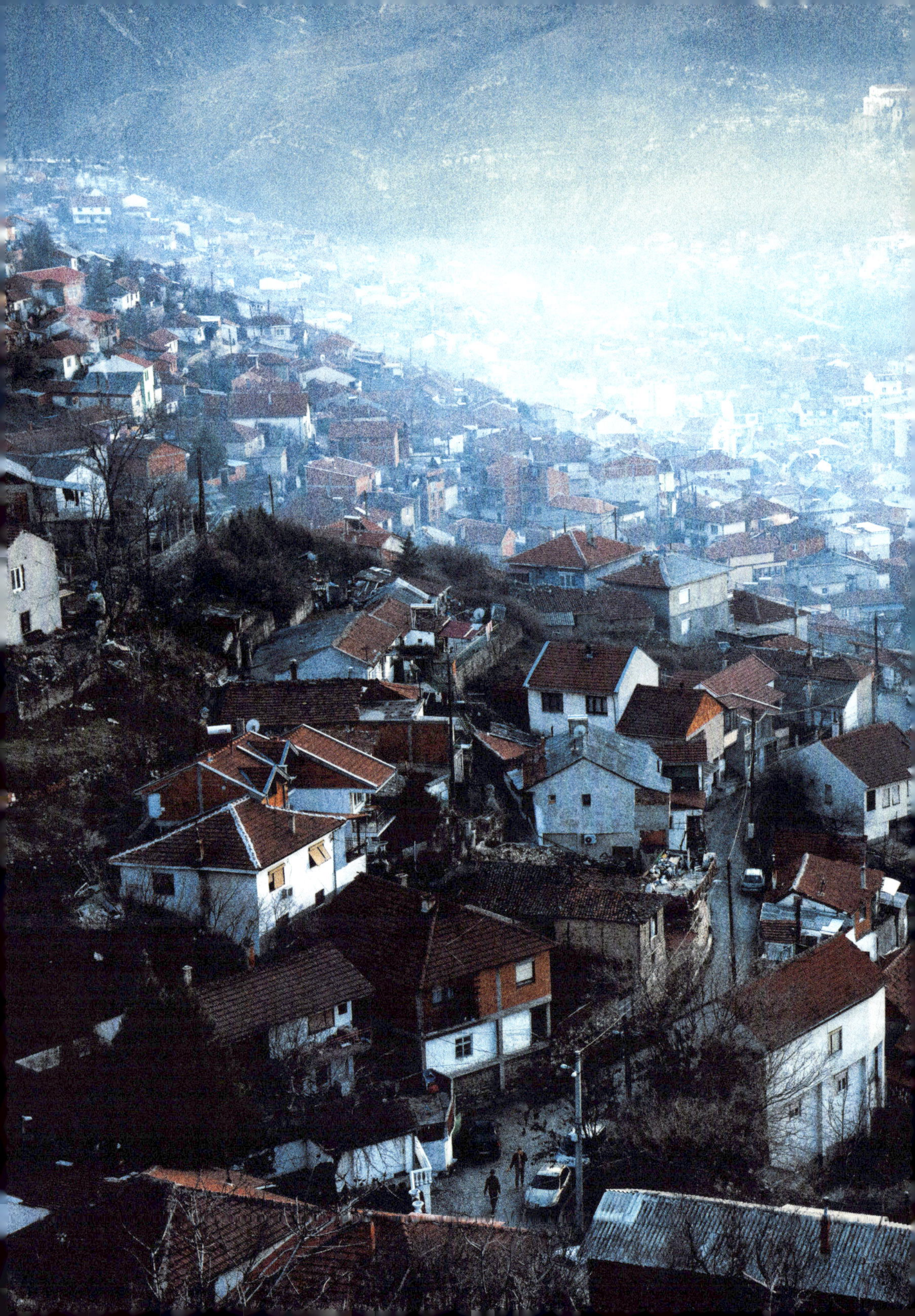

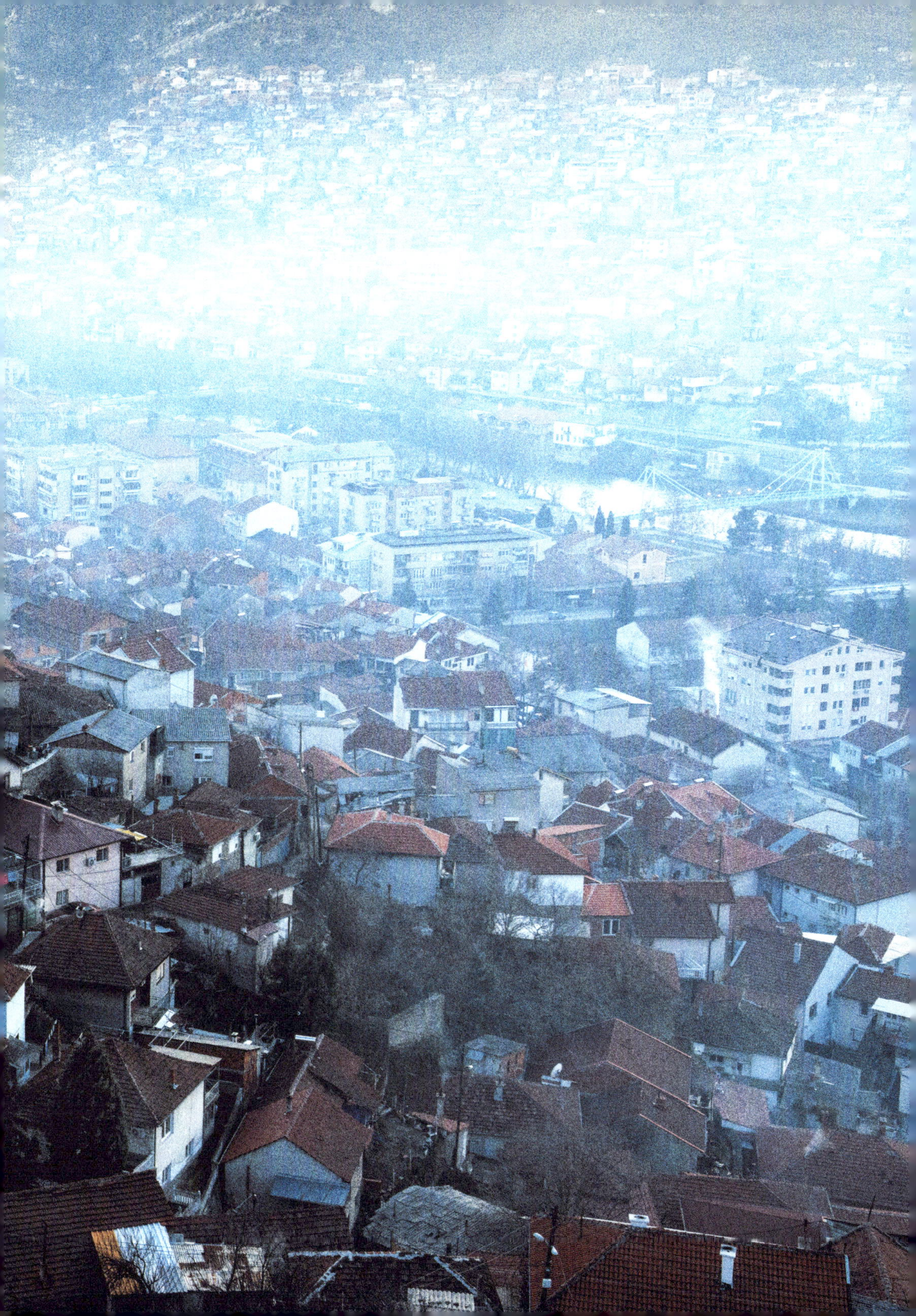

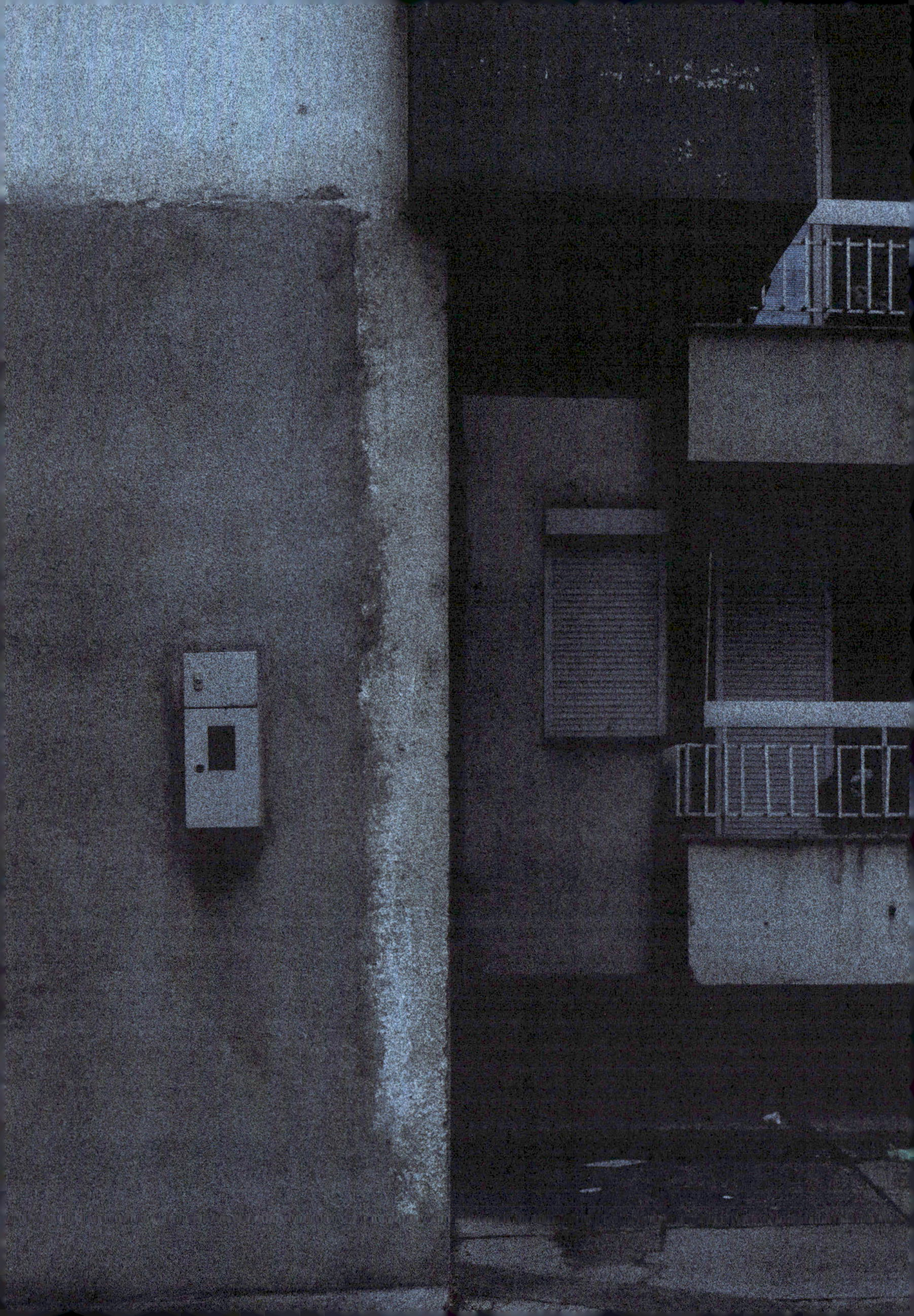

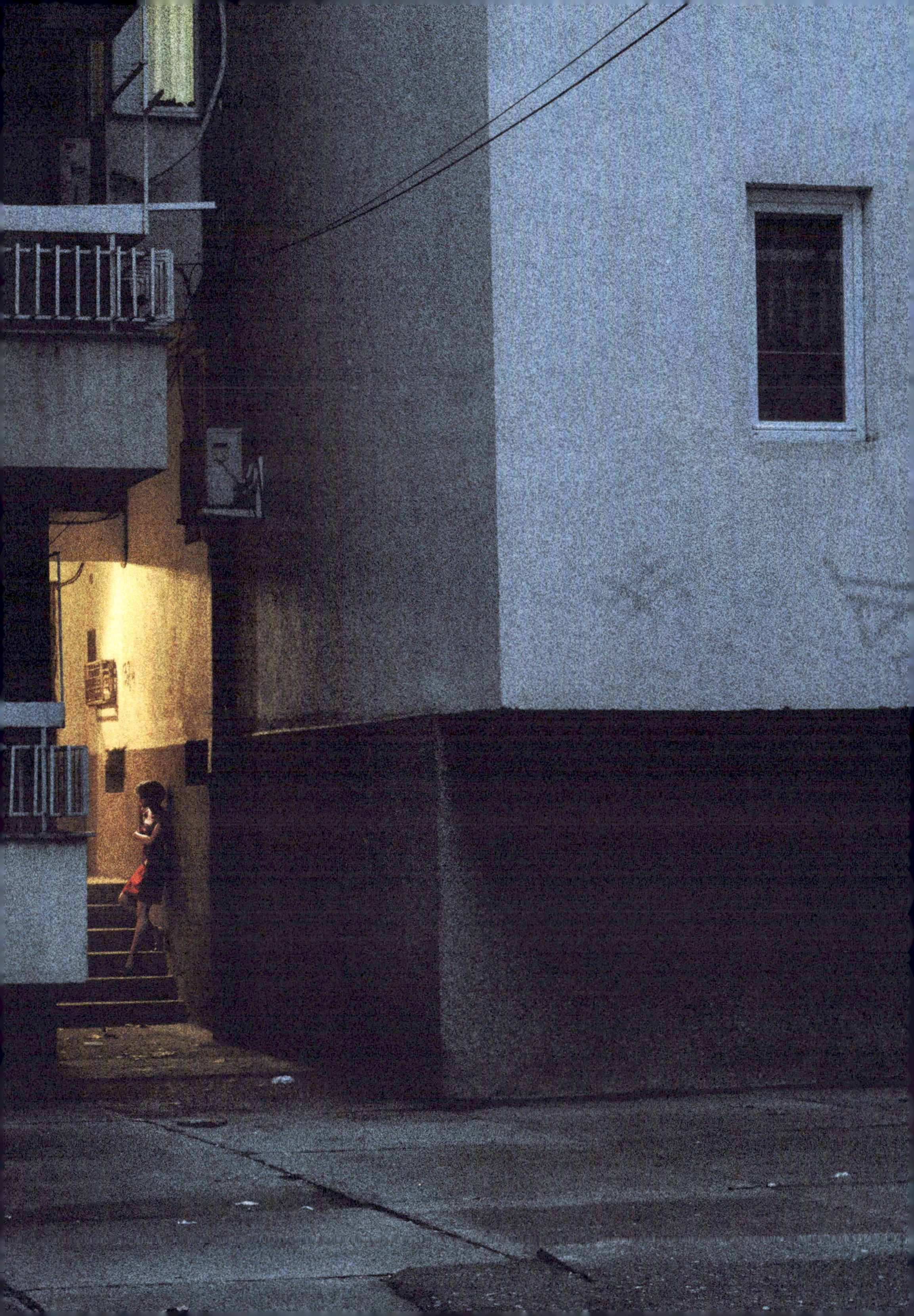

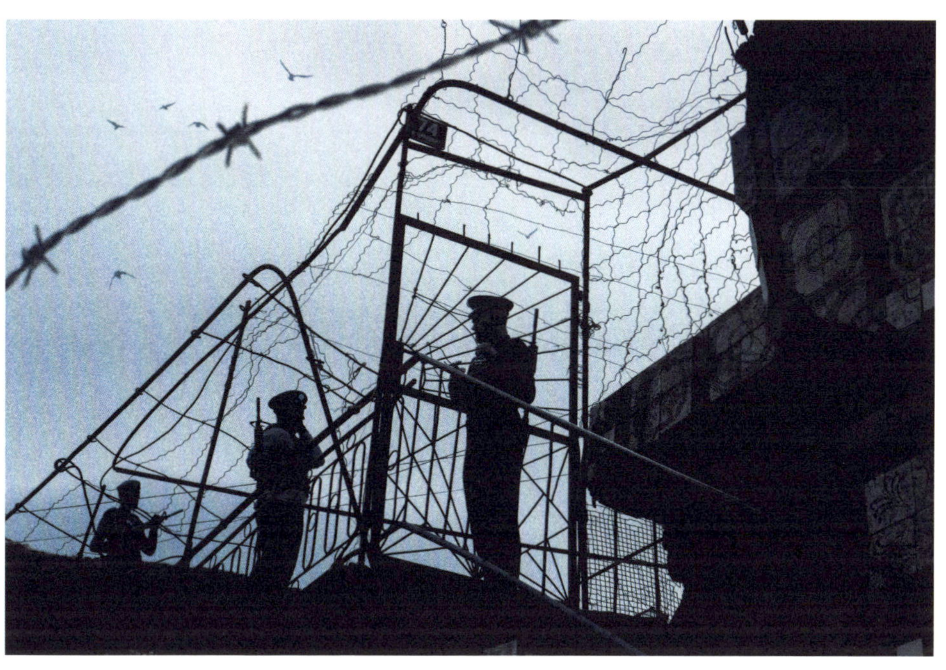

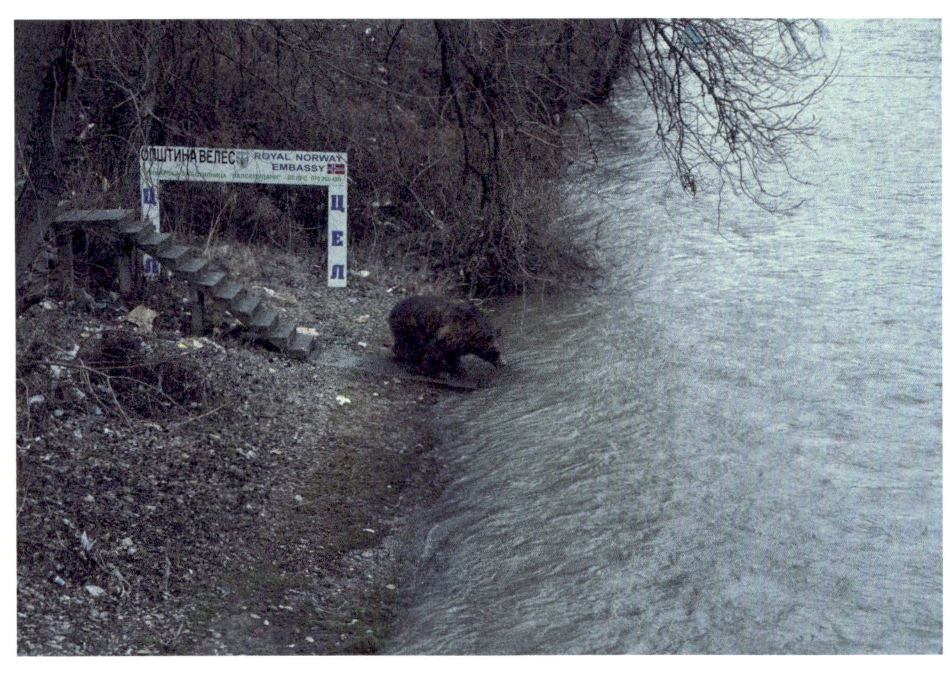

ОПШТИНА ВЕЛЕС
ROYAL NORWAY EMBASSY
ЦЕЛ
ЦЕЛ

B o a r d   3 1 - A (continued)   Part II

(...) but Veles (ВЕЛЕС) turned and said to them,

"These arrows and swords will not hurt you. And my lips will not speak falsehood. "

Upon saying all this, the young prince turned and saw a bear-god in the vision. And he was smitten with terror, and for the first time in his life he turned away from the ways of father Oriy (OPIE) and toward the ways of Veles.

***

And Tikhomir (ТИХОМИР), upon seeing the lie, was angry, and he struck at the earth. Later the lie was discovered and corrected, and the warriors returned to their steppes, swearing fealty to their new king. But the new king, upon seeing the return of his warriors, said:

"I have no authority to lead them after. They are princes of their tribe or clan, chosen from among their tribe-families. And here they stand before Veles, doing as is

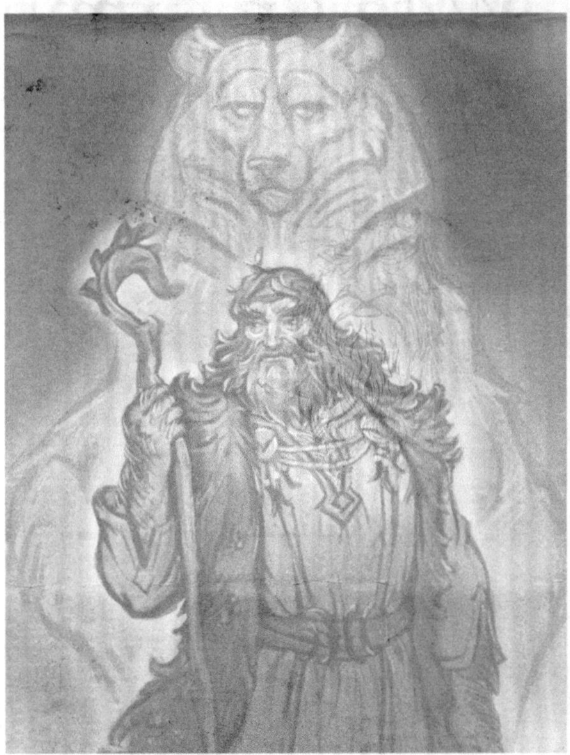

Veles in the shape of a bear. He is often depicted as
a bear on wood carvings and stonework throughout
the Slavic-speaking world.

(Artwork by Masha Kuravcova)

*Project Veritas
Reveals How Hillary
Broke The Law
With An Army
Of People Dressed
As Ducks*

www.USconservativetoday.com

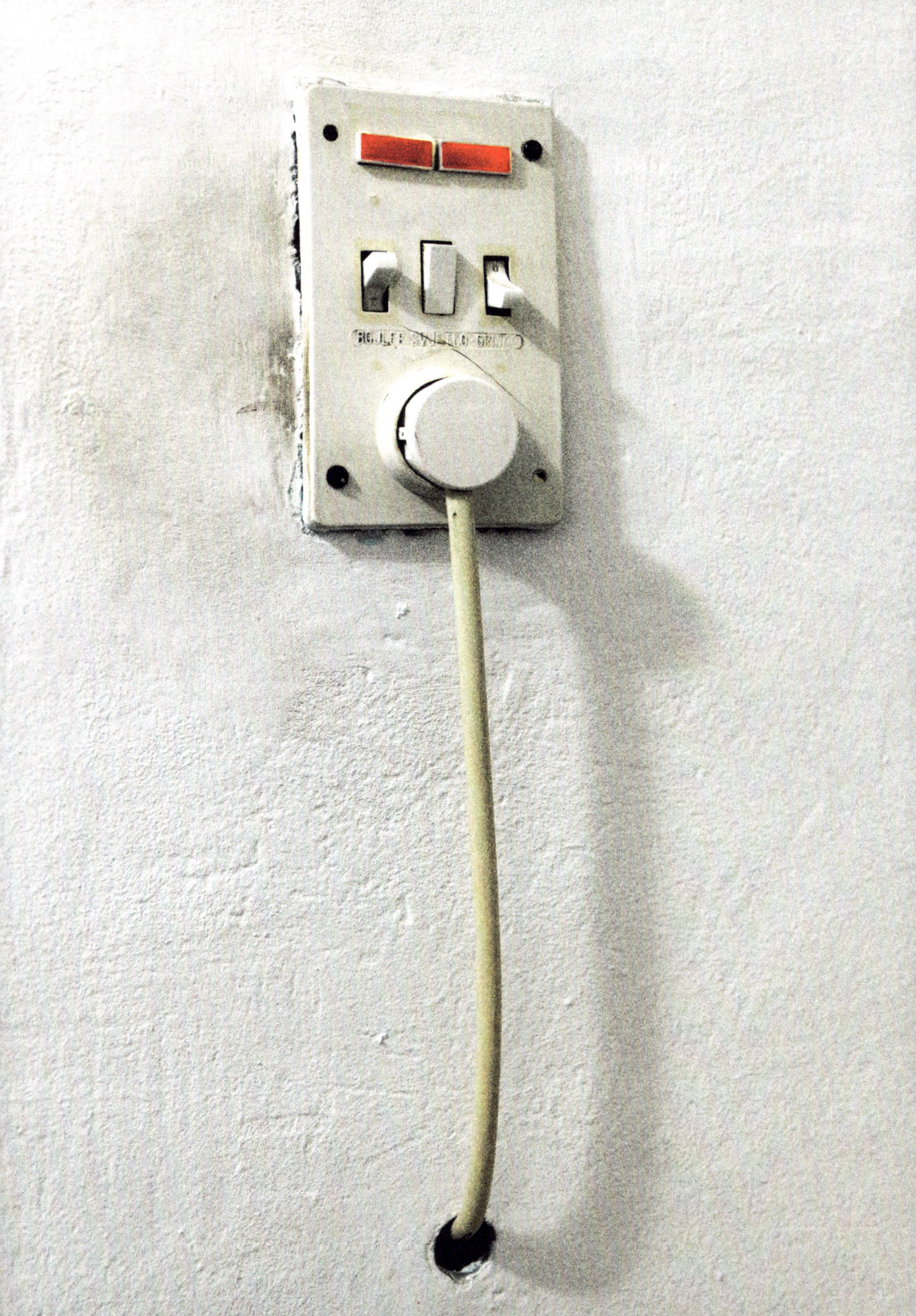

BOILER   IMMERSION   GRILL

"There is no moral
superiority. Our beliefs
do not define us."

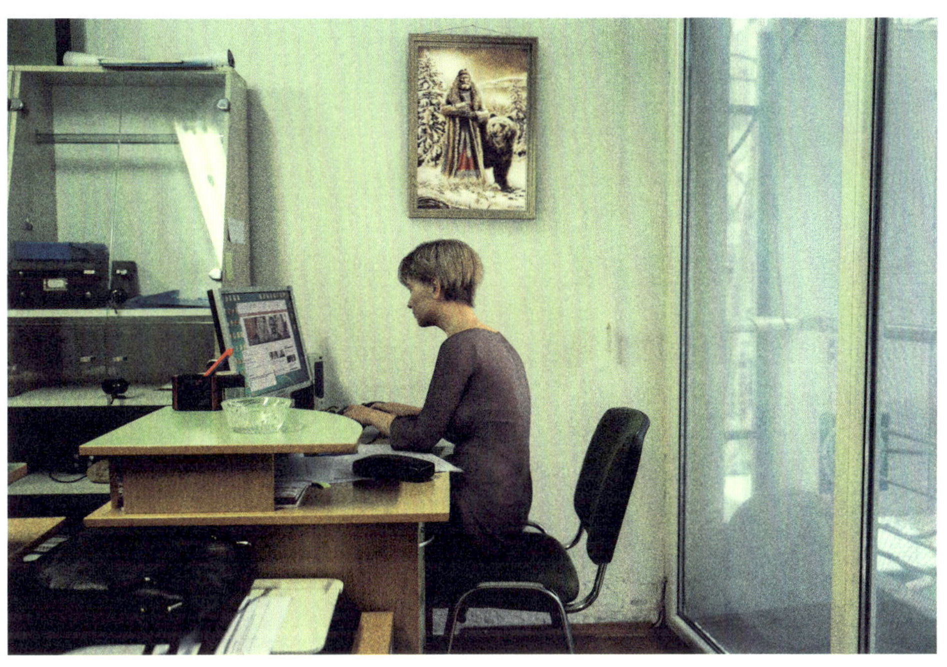

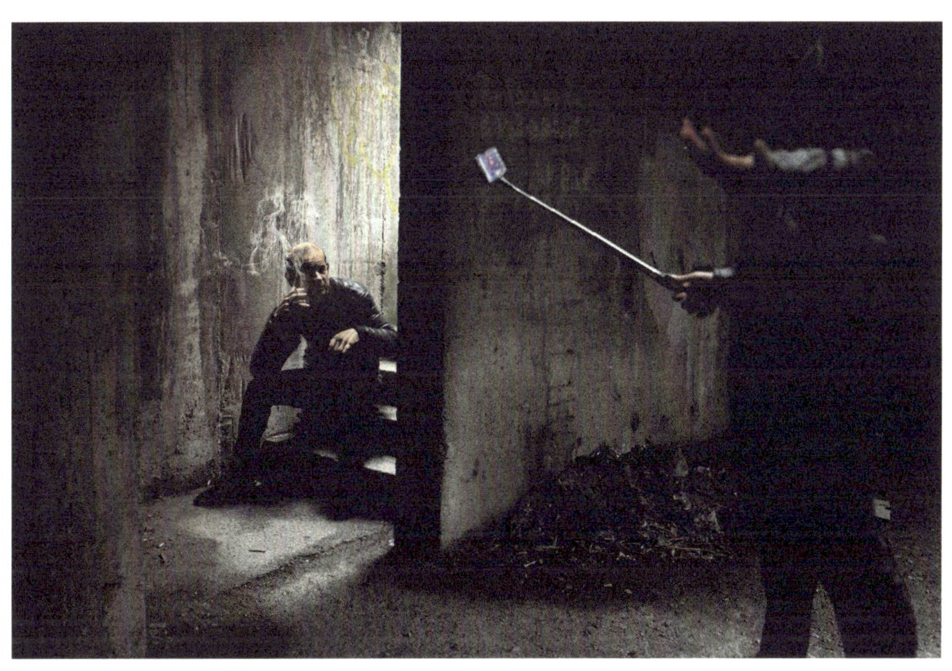

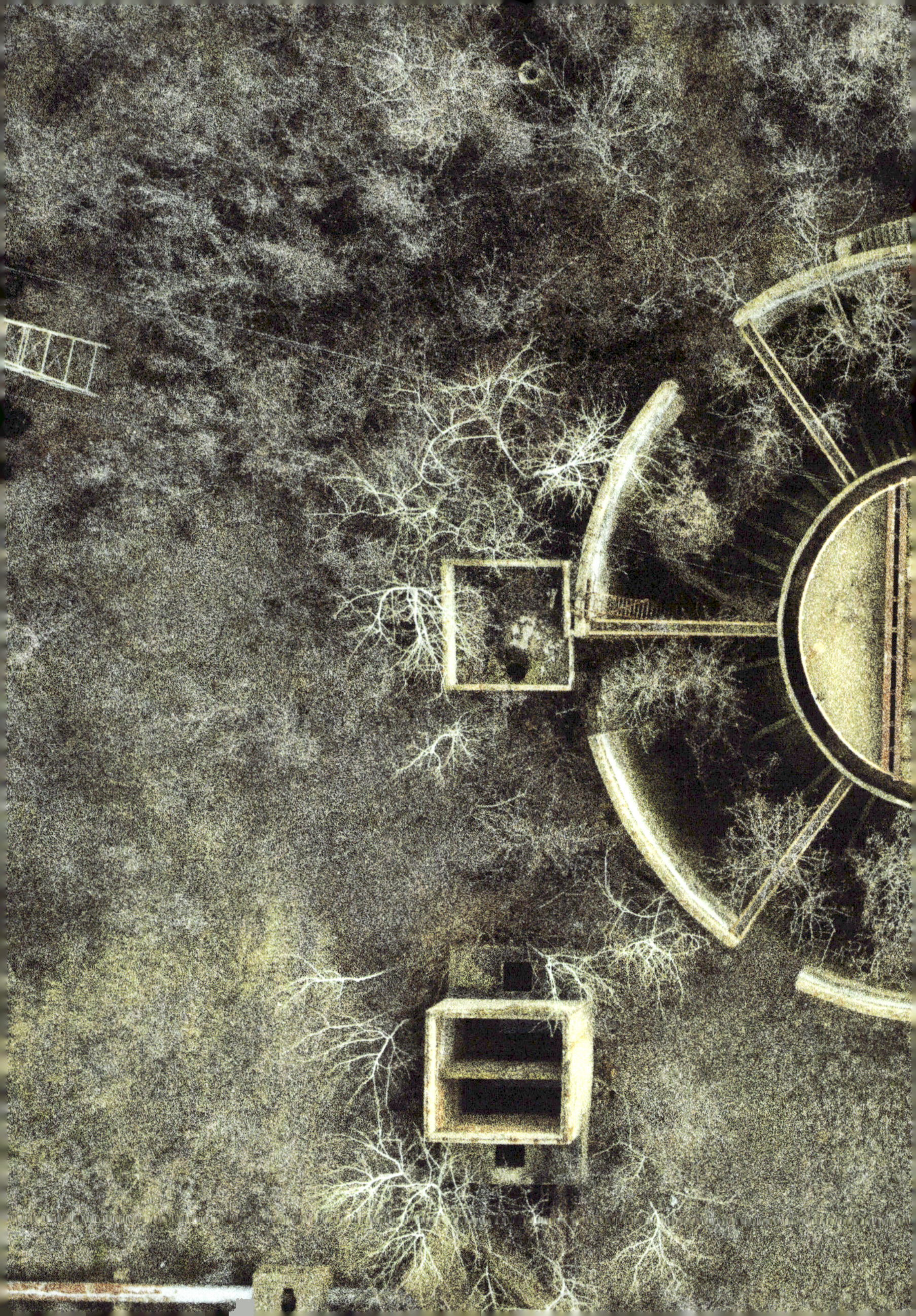

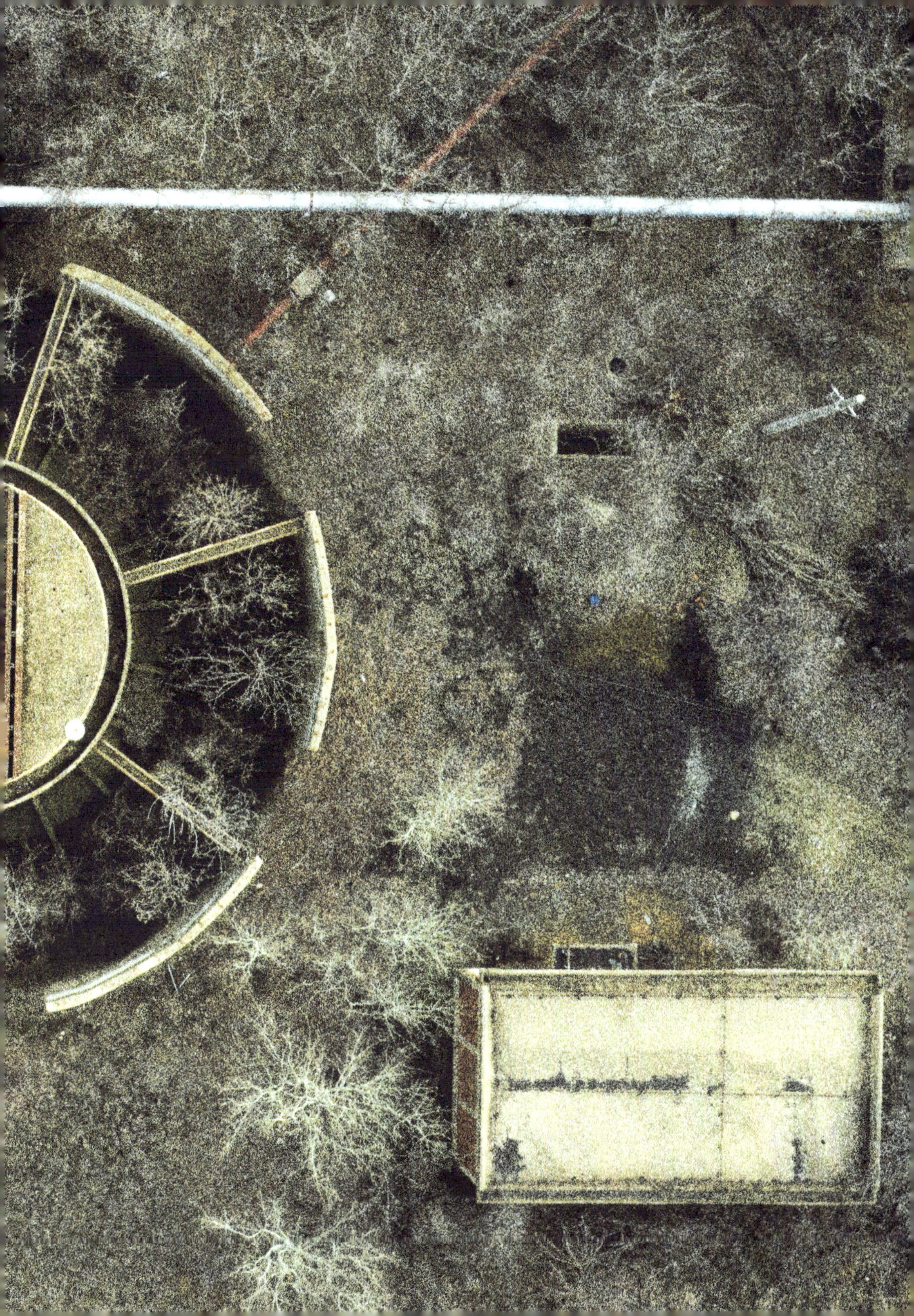

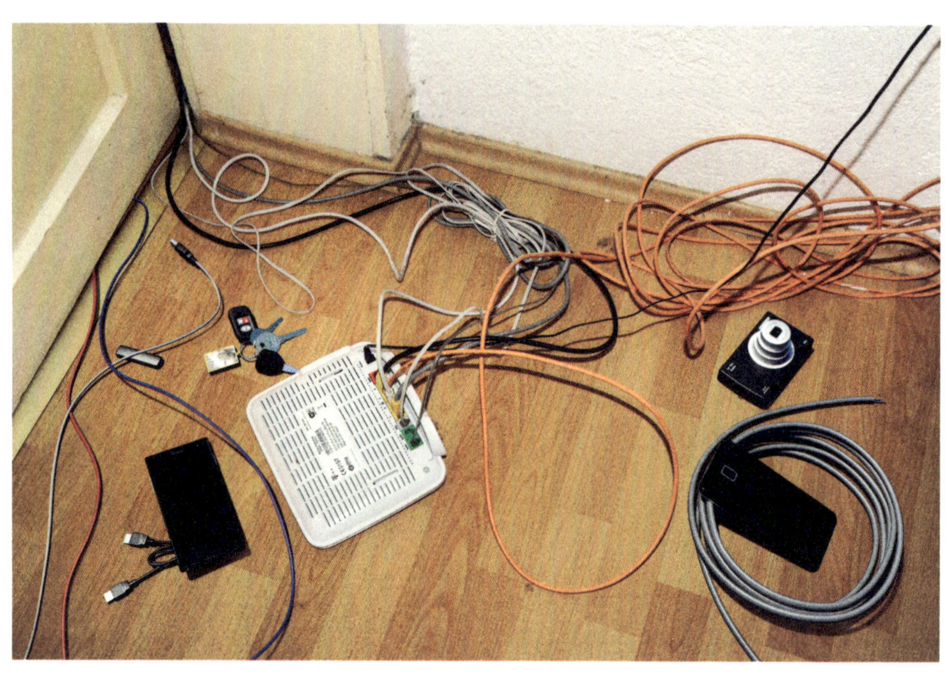

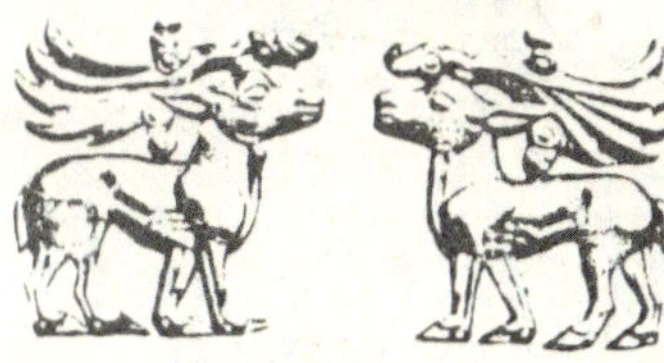

Part III

BOARD 9 - B

(40 lines of text)

As the battle drew near, Peroun (ПЕРУН) arrived, and Veles, thinking that Peroun was about to slay him, fled. But Peroun couldn't get through the forest and came to a small river. And when Veles saw that the god had not departed from the forest, went up to him and said:

"I am glad you have come to me."

"O Veles! I have come to ask you, the god of the forest, why you have taken my wife and my cattle. I ask that you give me back these things. I will not fight you. "

"O Peroun! Do you dare to ask me about the cattle?"

And Peroun was angry.

"Let us fight with all our might!"

Veles was still angered, and he used his powers to change into his warrior form. Peroun then said to Veles, "I will slay you!"

And so they fought. And there it was that fierce battle went on for ninety days.

And Peroun was the more brave, but the god Veles was the more powerful. Then the god Peroun asked the god of the earth (БОГ ЗЕМЛИ), "Who is the best of them all?" and the god of the earth answered, "The best of them all is Veles."

And Veles killed Peroun.

Note:

While the early Slavs were polytheists, and worshipped a number of different deities, the only two gods that were commonly respected and worshipped by all the Slavic tribes were Veles and Peroun.

Veles and Peroun are the two most powerful gods in the Slavic pantheon, and continually in conflict with one another.

The reason for the enmity between the two gods is Veles's theft of Perun's son, wife, or, usually, cattle. It is also an act of challenge: Veles, in the form of a huge serpent, slithers from the caves of the underworld and coils upwards the Slavic world tree towards Perun's heavenly domain. Perun retaliates and attacks Veles with his lightning bolts. Veles flees, hiding or transforming himself into trees, animals or people.

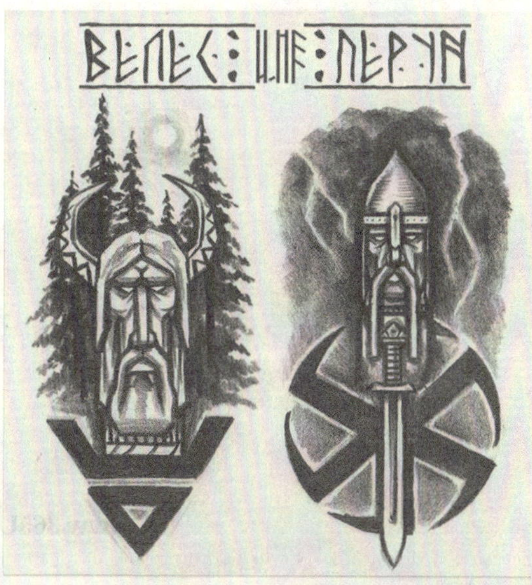

MUST-WATCH: In 120 Seconds You Will Be Voting For Donald Trump! OH YES!

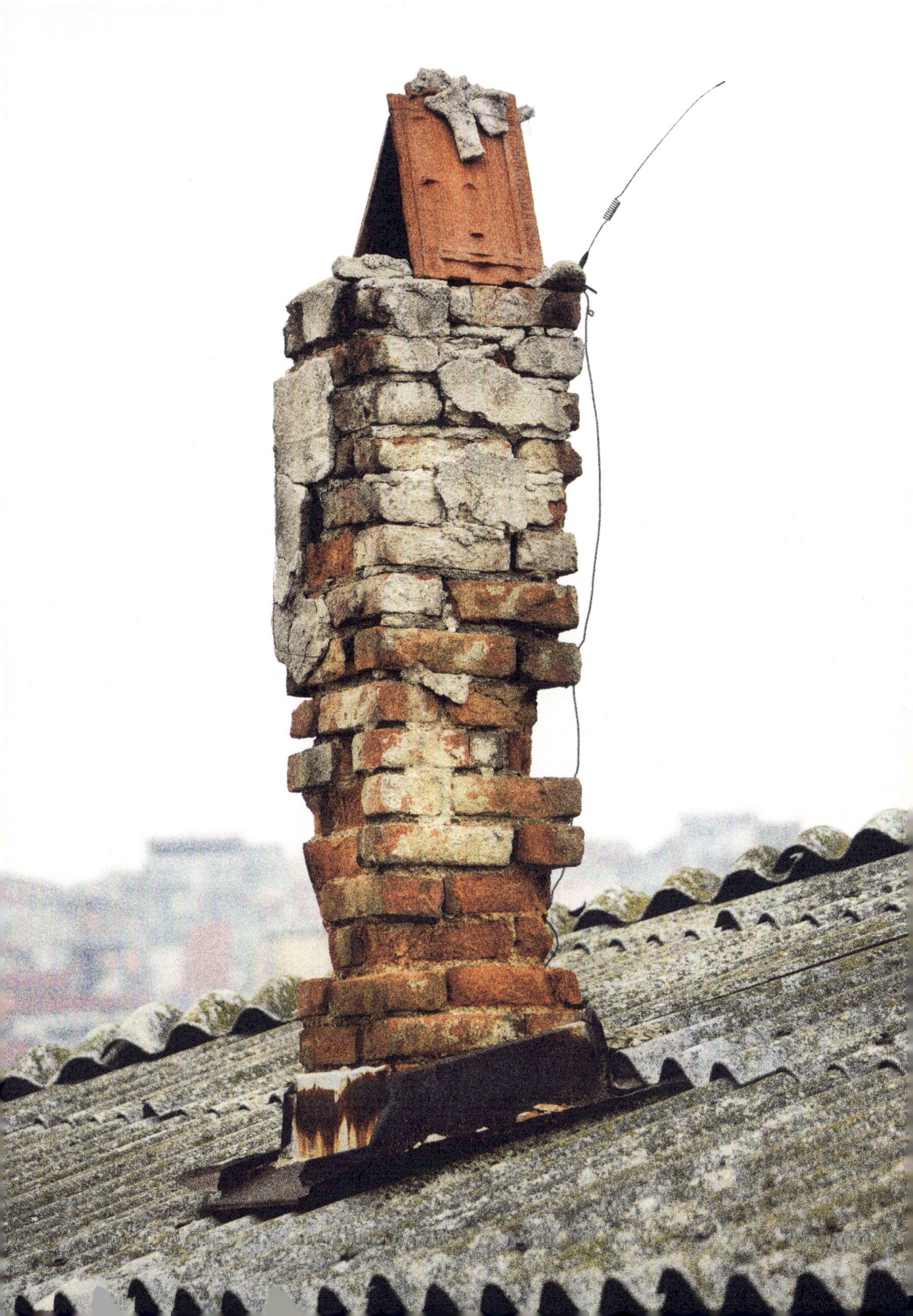

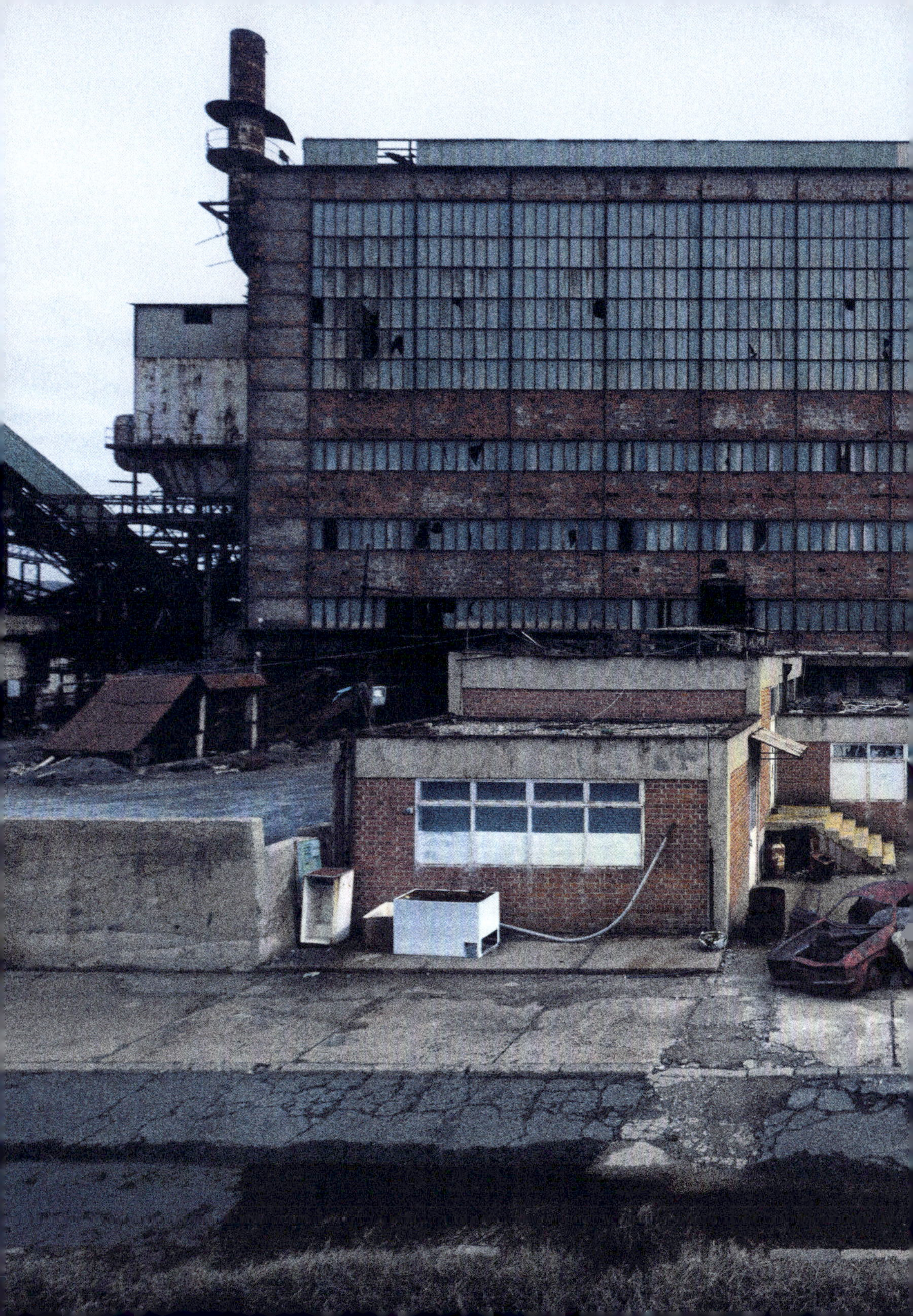

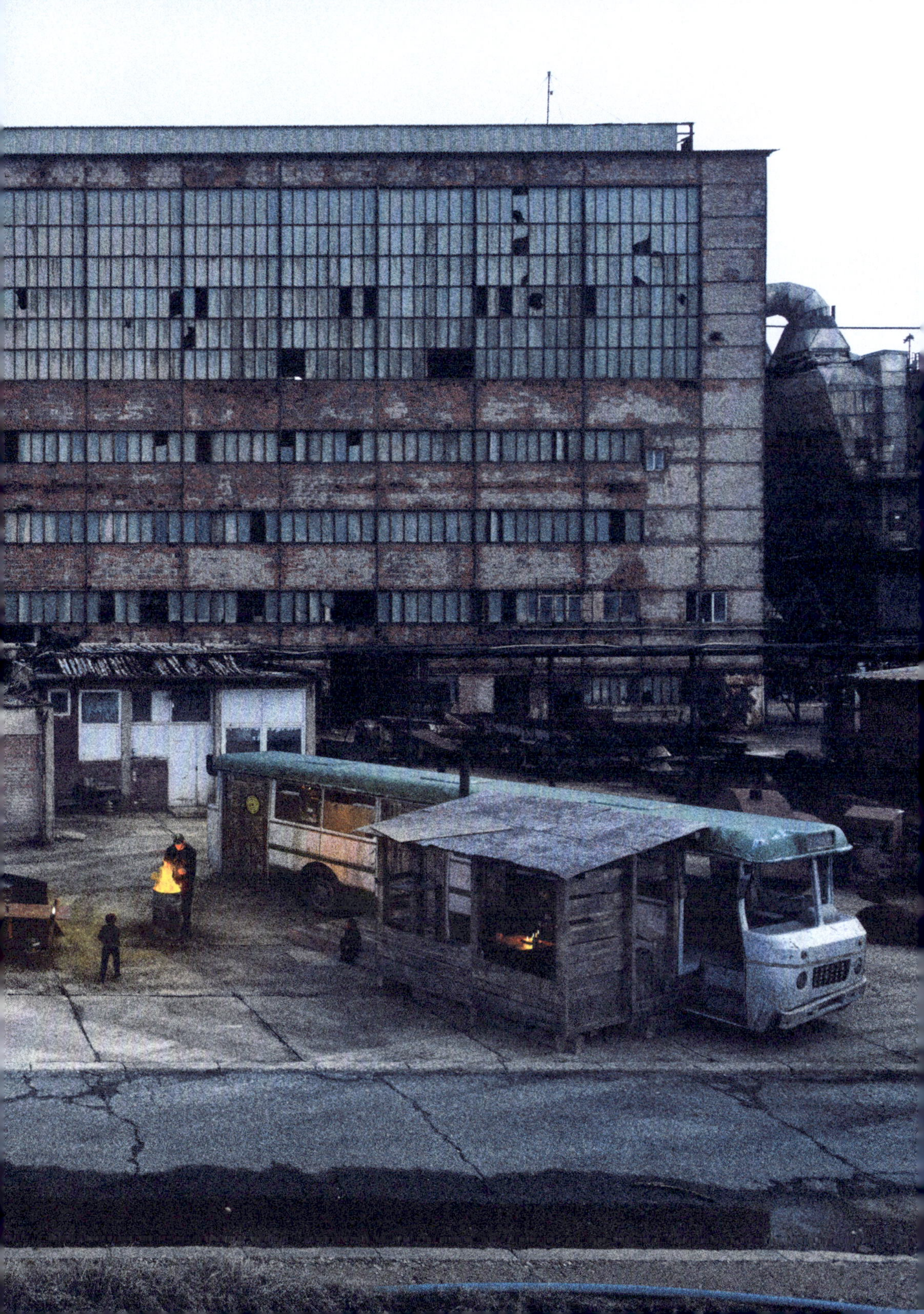

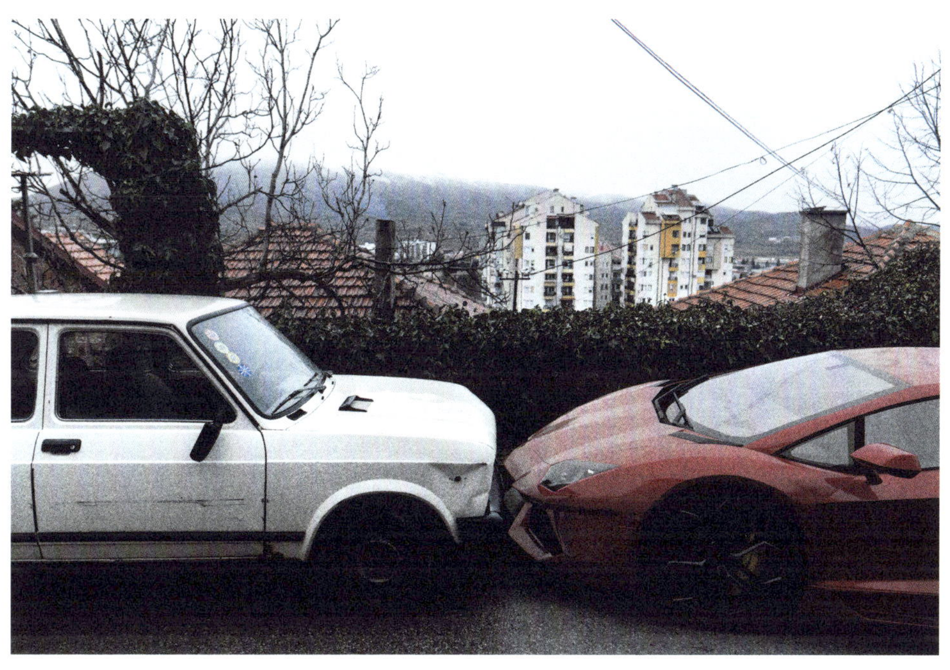

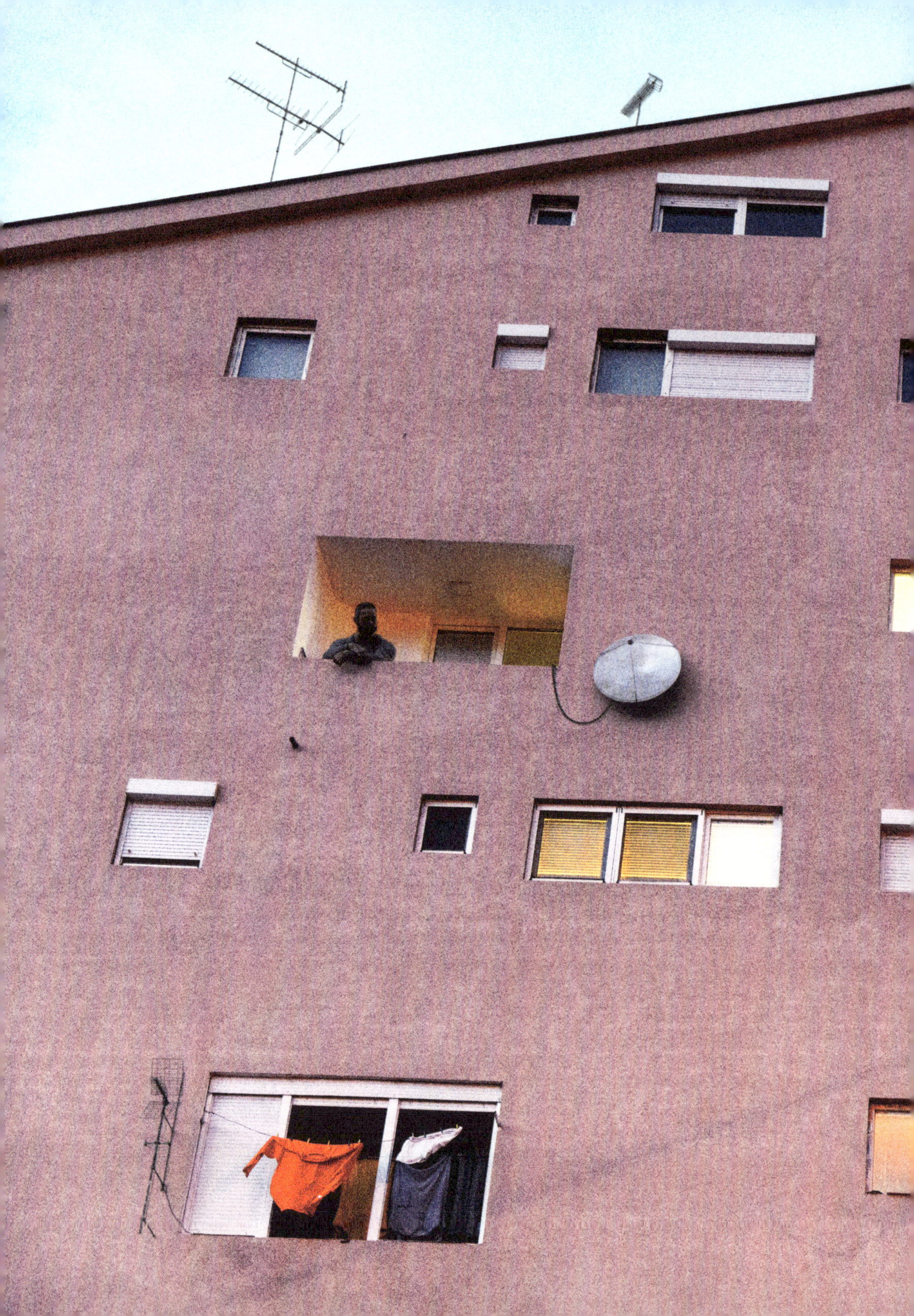

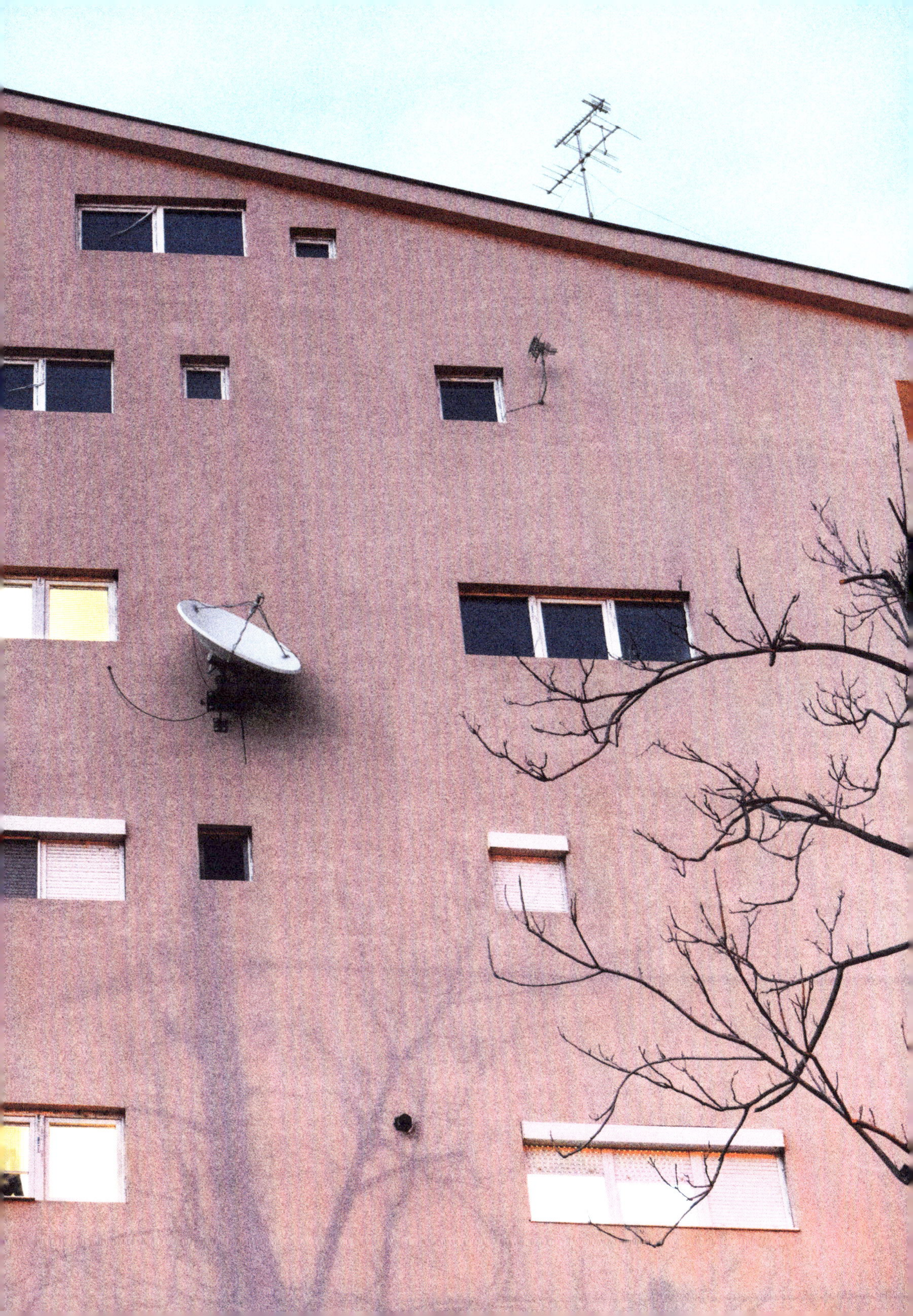

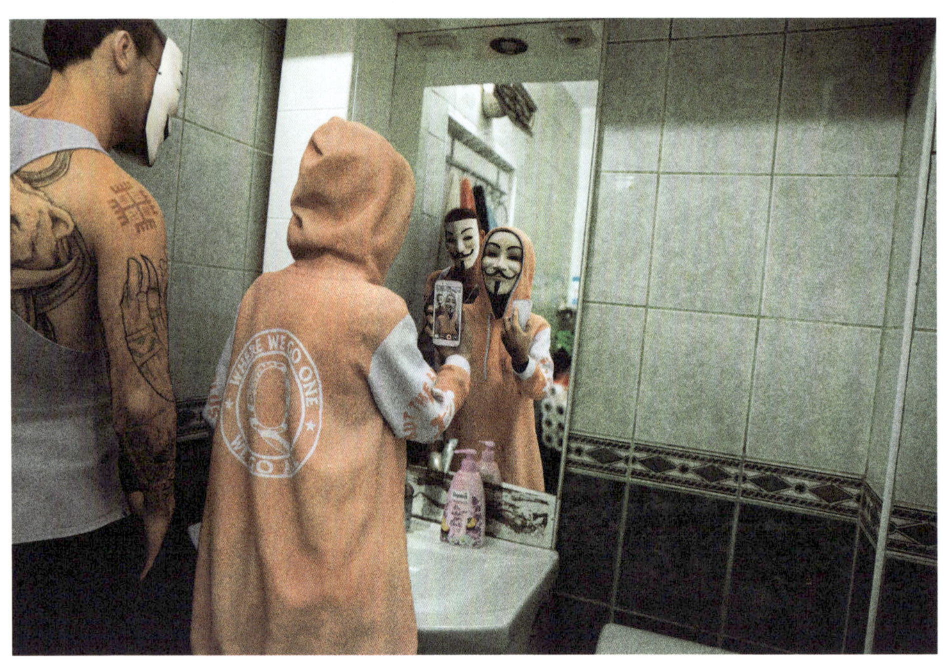
WHERE WE GO ONE

For those are such priests (ЖРЕЧIE) who tell us (= say) to bow to their god (?), but then they will steal from him.

We do not have them now, for we do not have falsehood. Our warriors are true to the end, and we from the beginning.

This is what we teach our sons about the bravery. And this we also teach our daughters about the success in this way of life. And here we see how truth comes to us through reason. And this we have to apply to our own cases. For the gods tell us:

"Walk toward Ruthenia (РYCE), and never after the ways of your enemies"

And it so happens that we have to accept it, for it is what is true.

And here we see the magicians from the forests, going up and down on the seven hills, who come to the seven winds of Veles (ВЕЛЕC). And this we learn from these warriors are the rulers of the land.

They wanted to rule over them, and took power over them. That is, we do not have a right to be at their head, because they have been transformed into wolves. Such a one, when he sees another, sees in him both the liar and the deceiver. He does not listen to the words of wisdom, only to the lying lips.

***

Mirrors are perpetually deceitful. They lie and steal your true self. They reveal only what your mind believes it sees.

Cleverness isn't always true nor is the truth always clever.

Yet fooled with hope, the people favor this deceit.

So we went away with that truth, and came to another land. There we saw

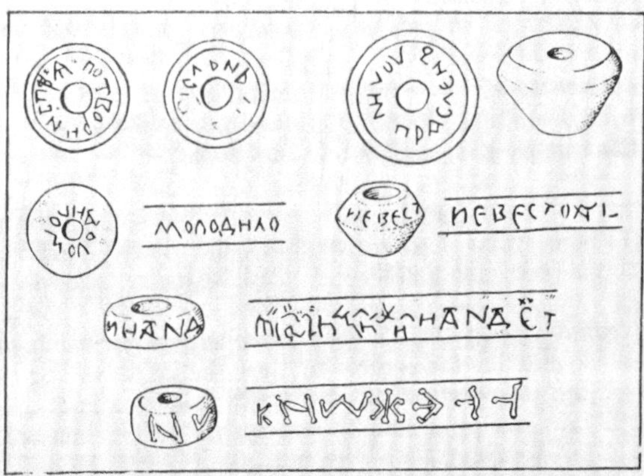

Надписи на русских пряслицах XI—XII вв.
(по Б. А. Рыбакову)

Samples of Ruthene writing from the 11-12th centuries AD.

Source: V. A. Istrin, <u>1100 Years of Slavic Alphabet</u>
(in Russian), Academy of Sciences of USSR, 1963

BREAKING:
Putin Just Issued An International Warrant For George Soros… He Wants Soros Dead Or…

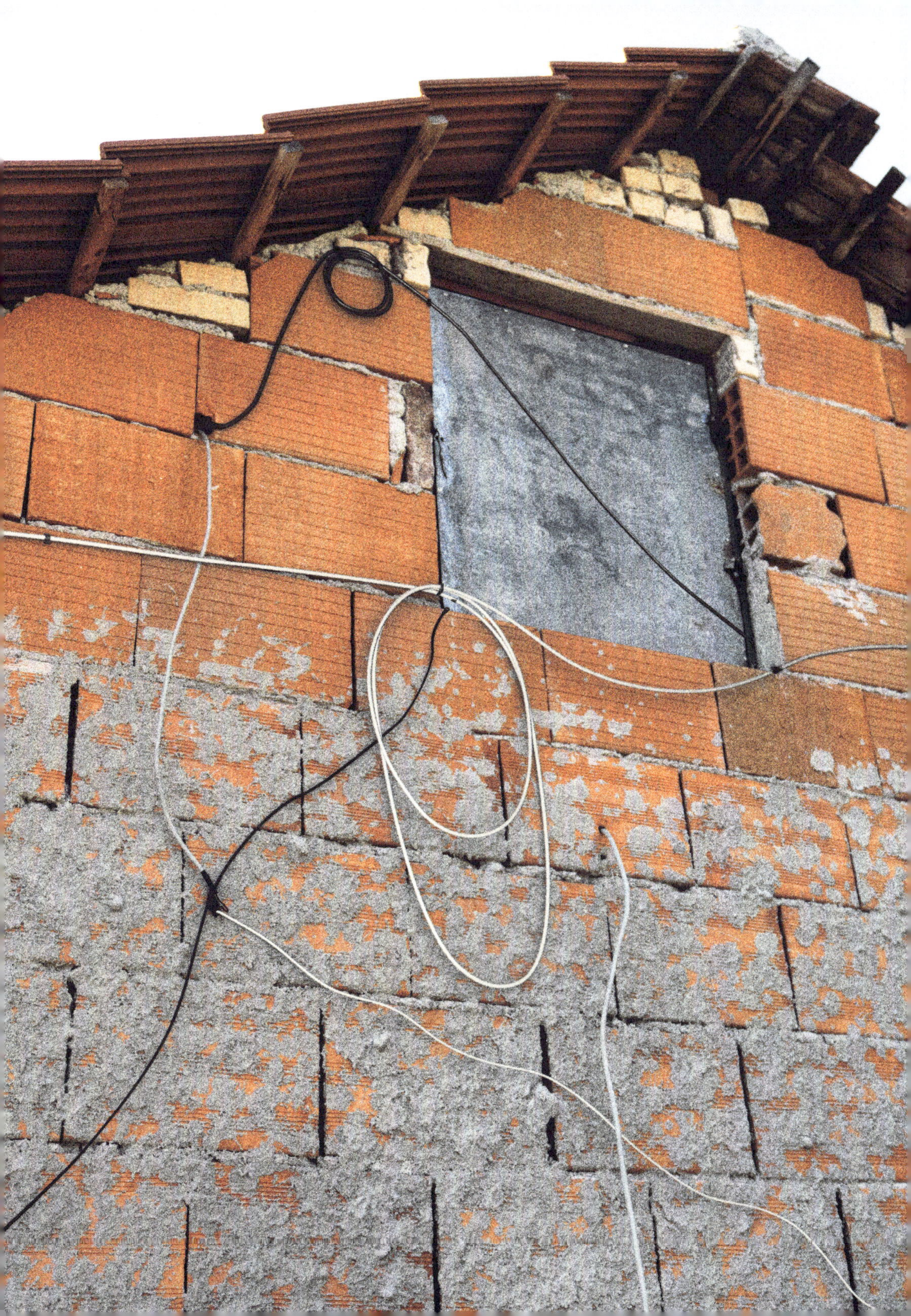

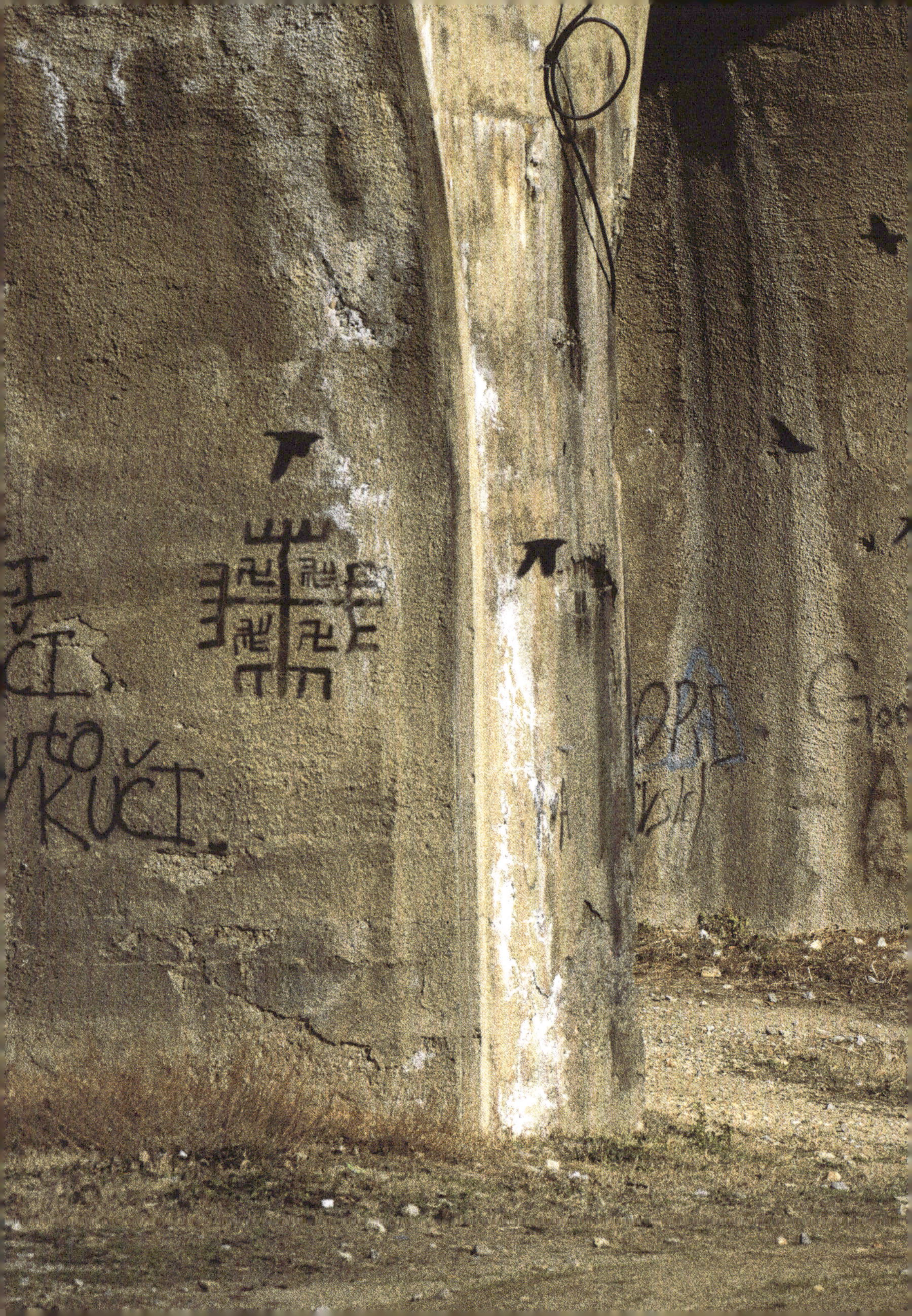

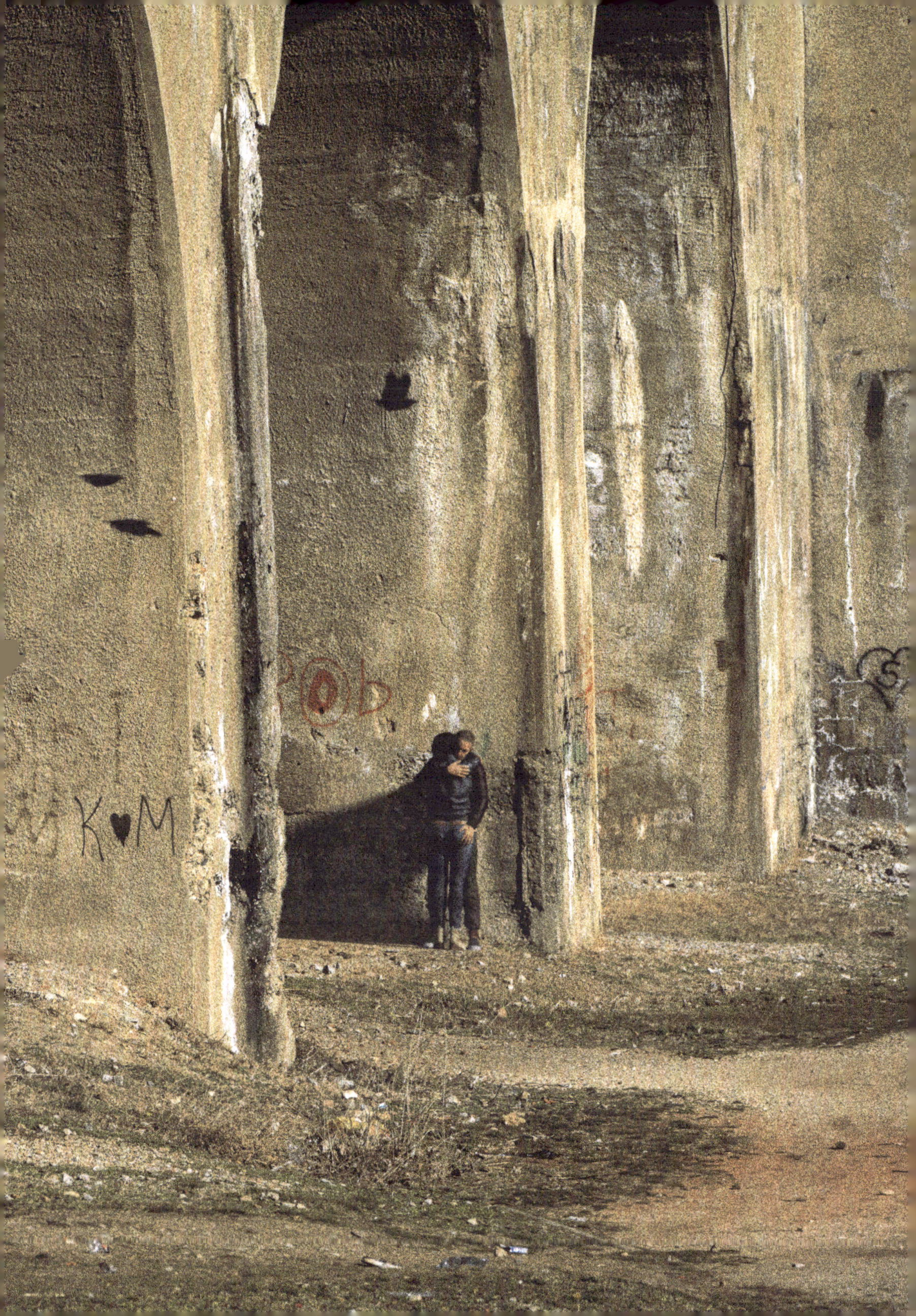

K ♥ M

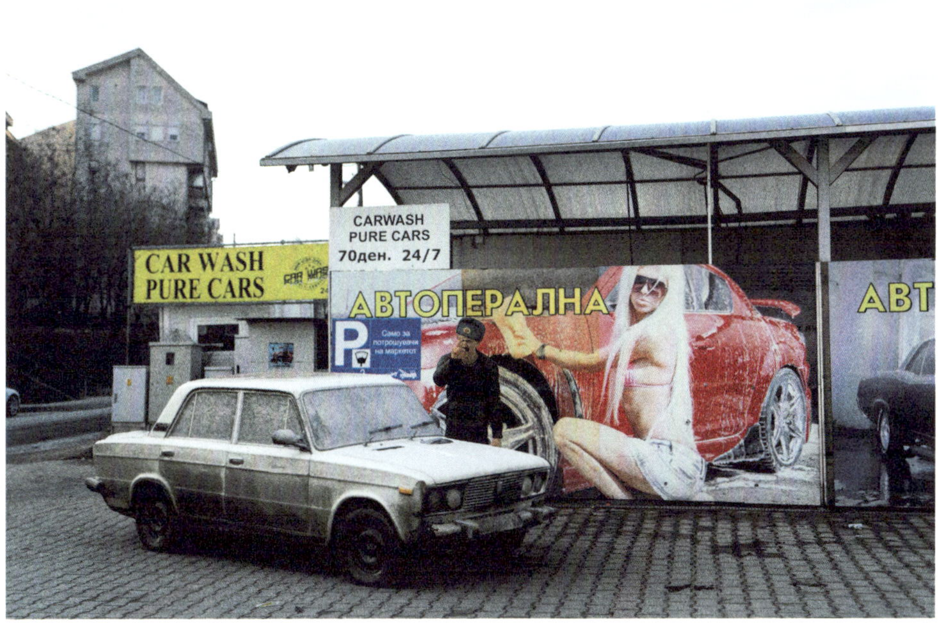
CAR WASH
PURE CARS
CARWASH
PURE CARS
70ден. 24/7
АВТОПЕРАЛНА
АВТ
P
Само за
потрошувачи
на маркетот

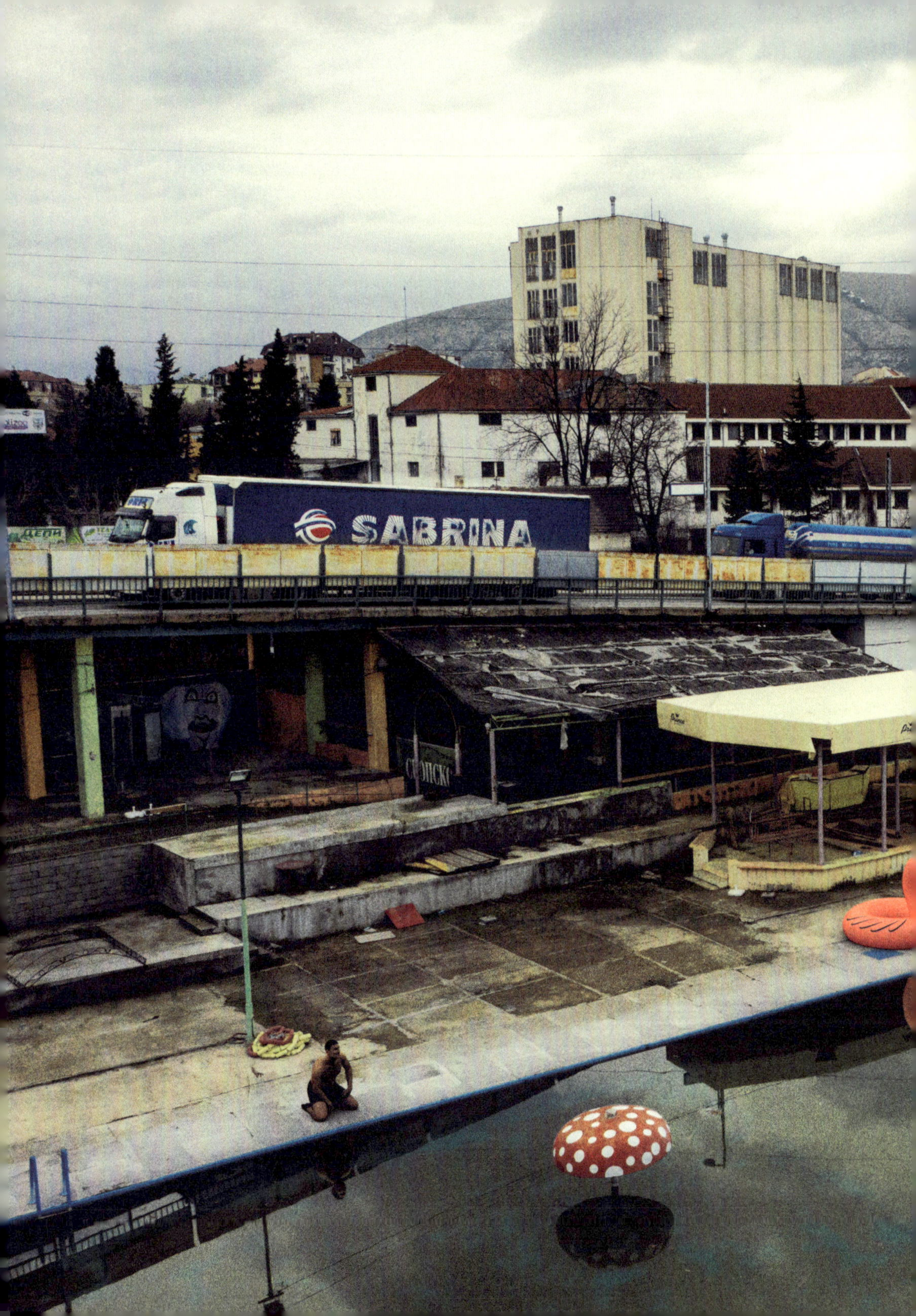

SABRINA

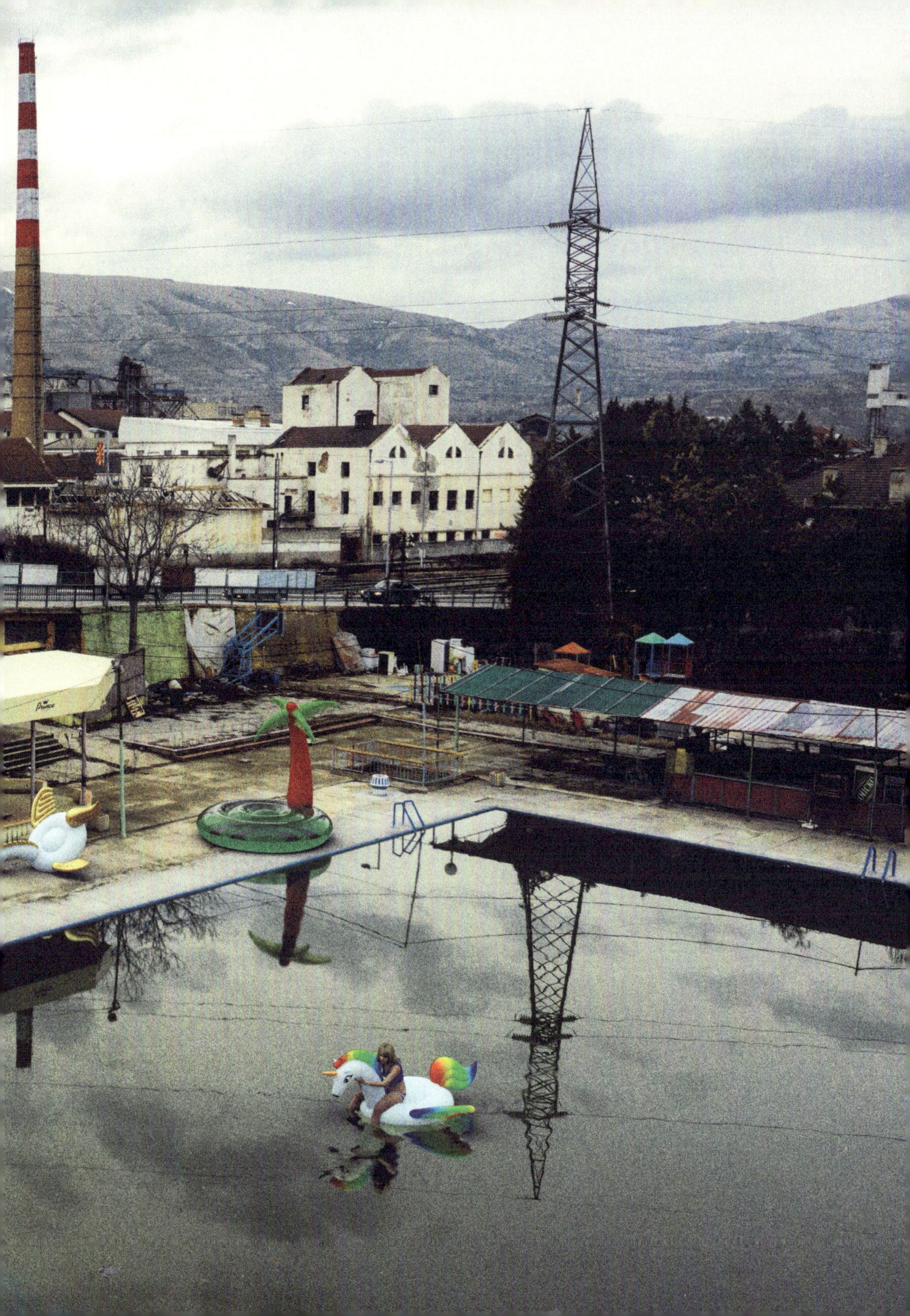

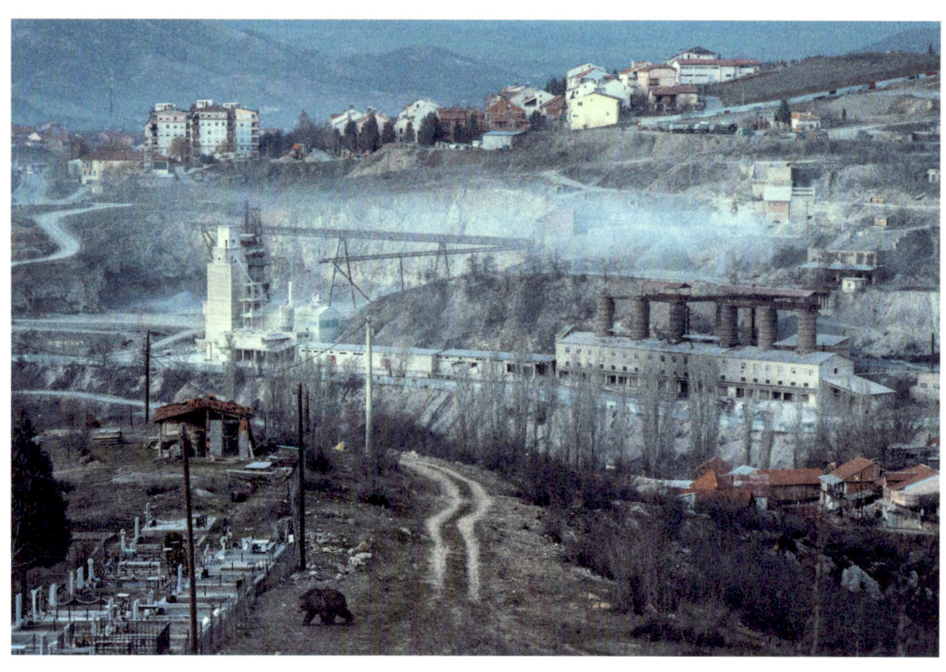

Then the god Veles (ВЕЛЕС) had his way -- And the godly power had appeared as a bear. Later the bear had turned and looked behind him, and saw that the Kievans were going south. And it turned back the godly power from there to his people.

But the god of Rus (БОГ РУСИ) then turned back said:

"Walk toward Ruthenia, And never after them."

Then the bear would have attacked them, and they would have lost their land and kin. But the God of Rus (БОГ РУСИ) said to continue.

The people of Veles then went northward, and thus encountered the Wei. And they defeated them. When the people saw this, they were amazed at the power of the beast, and also at the riches of life. And they decided to put away all else, and to go forth to the setting of the sun.

But the Matr Sva (MATOIPE CBA) Bird said:

"Let us go to the setting of the sun, for help will be there for us. And here we shall see many wonders, and the glory of the great Veles."

"For the hairy head of a bear is better than that of a witch".

"Better is it for us to perish today, than to endure for ever in the old life of slavery, servitude, and abuse. For this old life is of the vine, and it is better to die today than to endure in the old life of slavery, servitude, and abuse."

"For Veles had created us, and this old life is of the vine. Therefore, let us drink the surdrink (CYPE ПOITBY). This drink is for our strength, and it will be poured into the cup for our sustenance. And this drink is for our drink, and not for our bread. But the cattle will drink it, and the wine will be poured into it. And this drink will be as a water of life, in the last time of the great burial feast -- the one which is for all those who had perished defending their land."

***

This happened to Bohumir (БОГУМИР), the forefather by the bloodline, when he went to the setting of the sun. And he saw in the evening three men on horses, heading toward him.

"Who are you going to trust?" asks the Bear.

"I cannot rely upon my own strength, but rather upon the power of prophecy."

"And who are these three men on horses for Veles? For there goes Peroun' and there the Bear thunders in the bright sky, for that is the way of prophecy that leads to the shore."

And then the Bear sets out on a journey himself. And he arrives to a solitary oak tree that stands in the steppe, and stops there for the night, near his campfire.

*Biggest Presidential
Election Rigging In History
Discovered Against
Trump In 16 States*

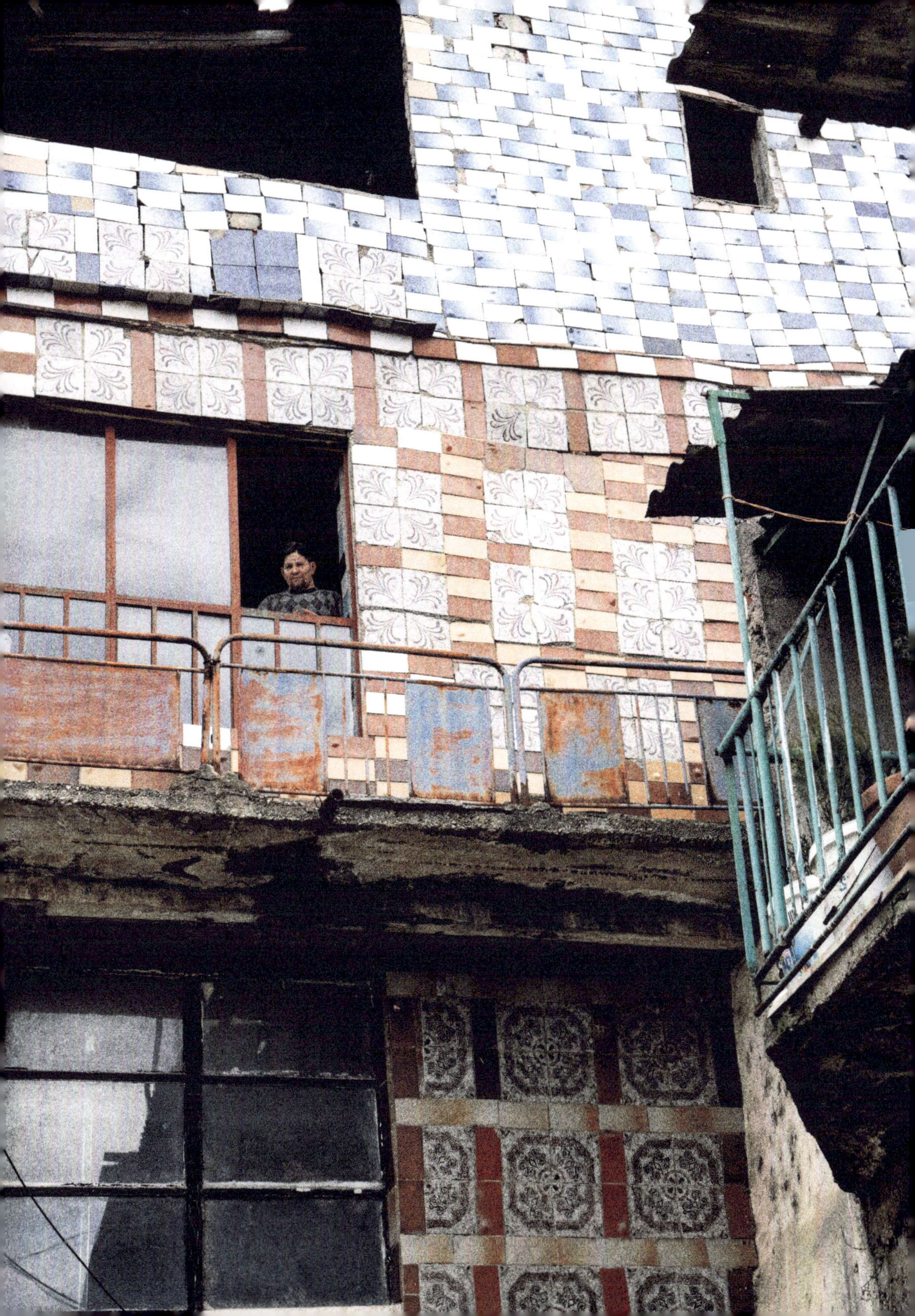

"There is no work here
that pays more than this.
It's not a real job, but it
is real money."

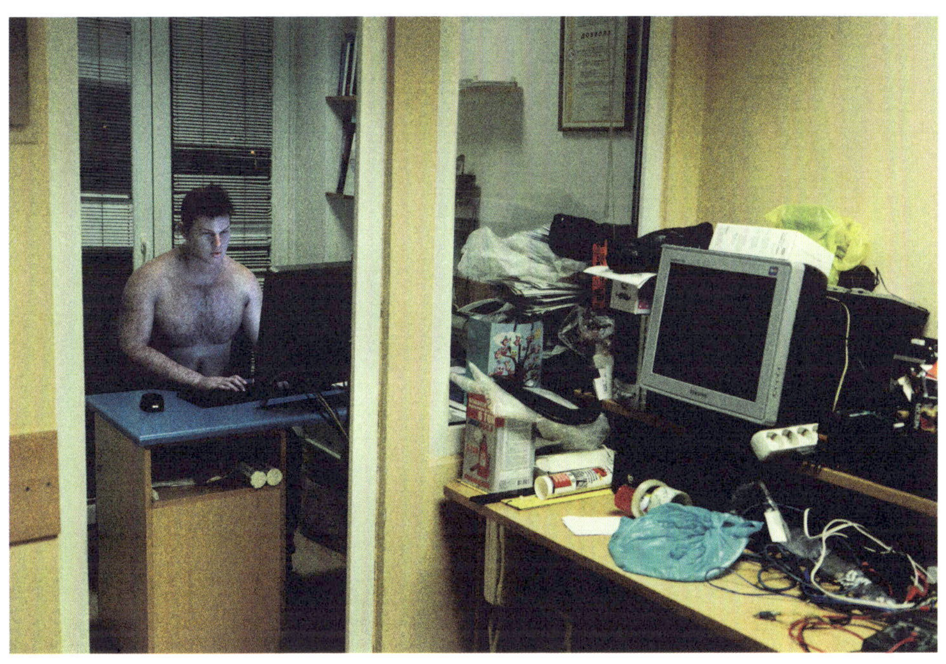

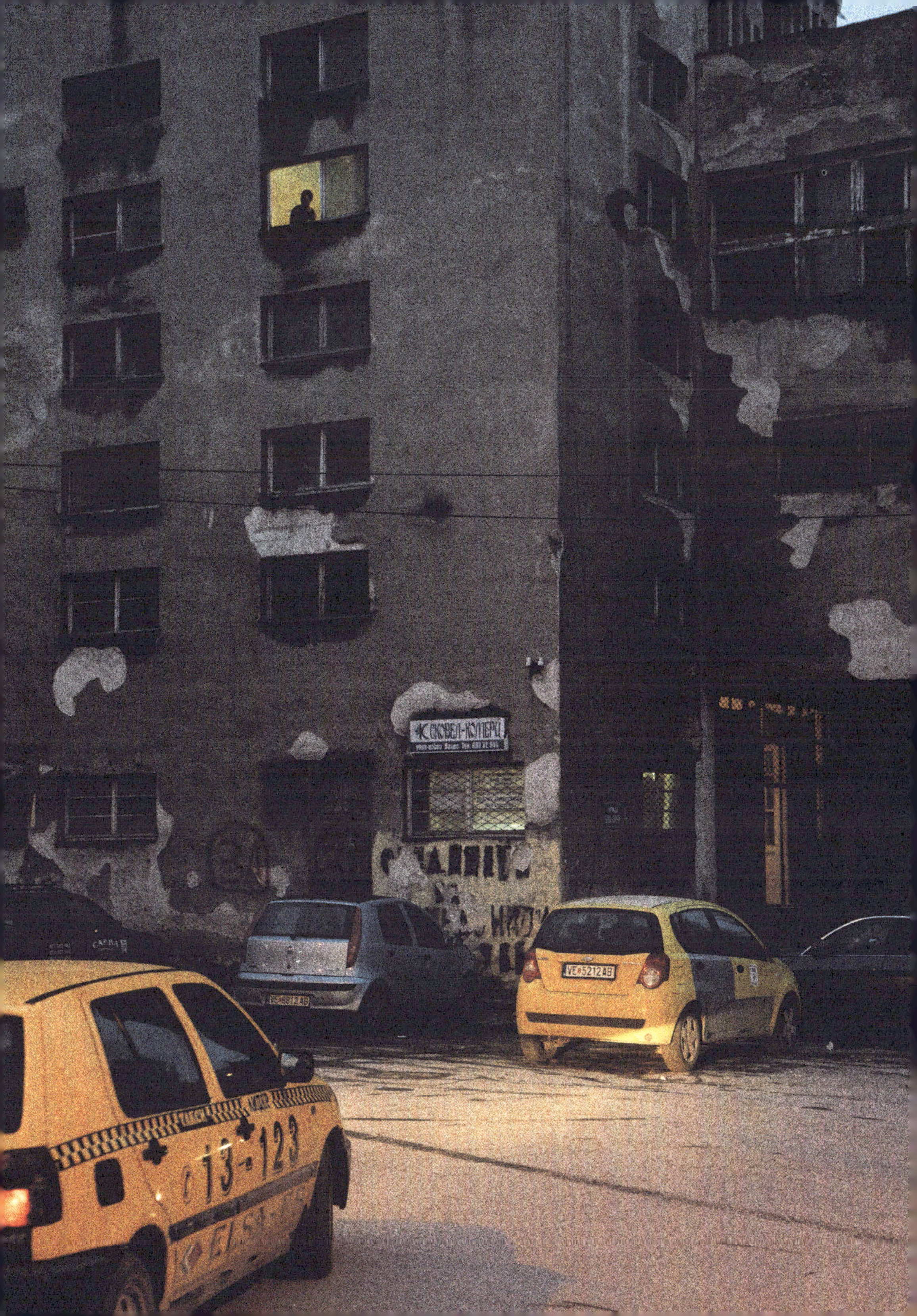
СКОВЕЛ-КОМПЕРЦ
VE 5212 AB
13-123

"Of course the media are corrupt. I hate to break it to you, but you are the enemy."

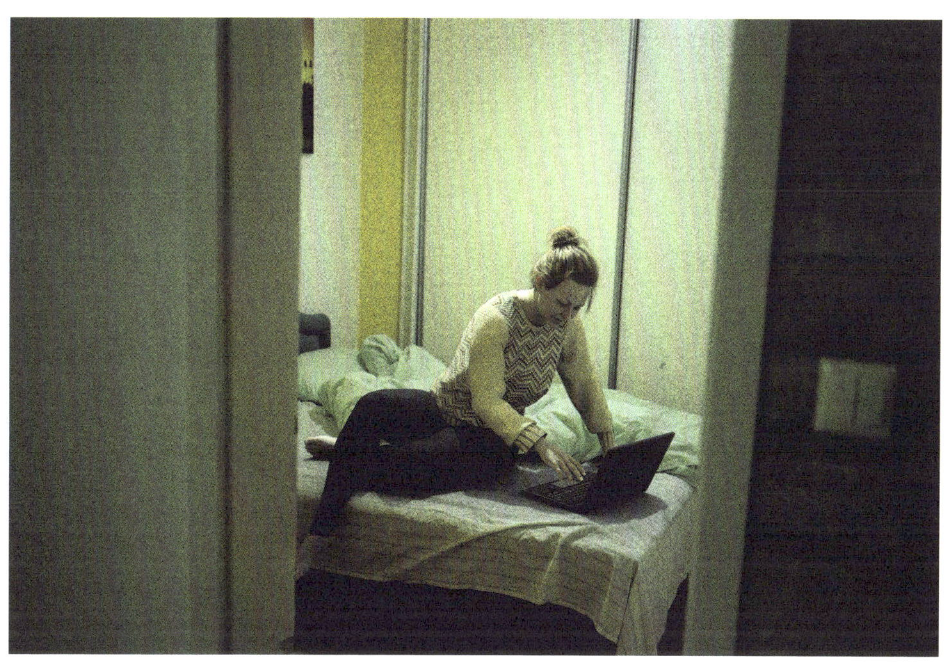

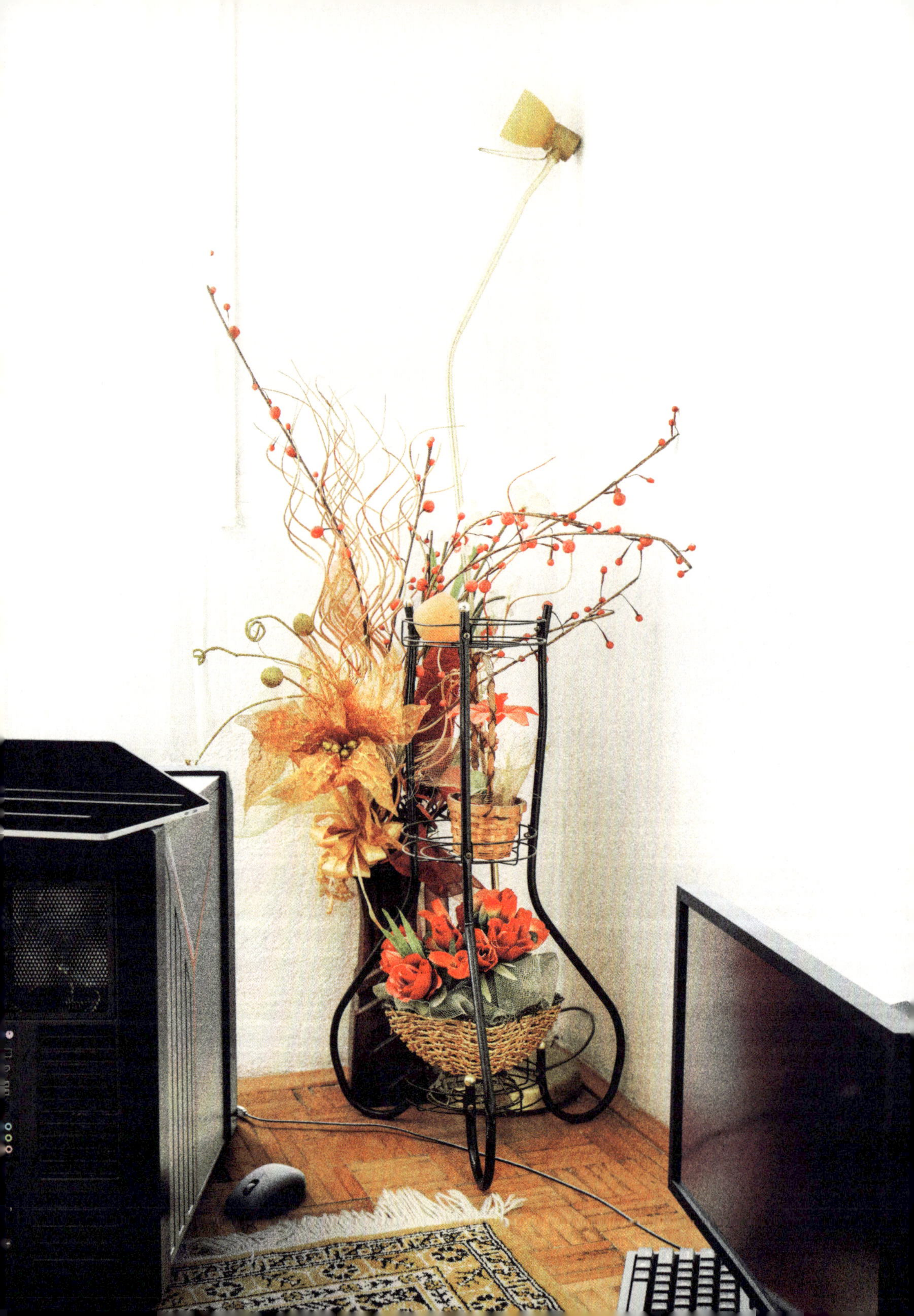

(continued)

At night, Veles (ВЛЕС) walks in the sky upon the Milk of
Heaven (that is, The Milky Way). And he goes to his palace, and
at the star-dawn (?) returns to the gates. There and then we
await to begin our songs, and to praise Veles (ВЛЕСА) from age to
age, together with his temple, which glistens with many fires,
and is a pure fire-hearth (?).

It was Veles who taught our ancestors how to plow the
soil, and plant the grain-seed, and to harvest the grain-spikes
in the fields of labor; and to bring the grain-sheaf into the
hearth-house, and to respect him greatly (?) as a godly ancestor.

Here even the bears[3] have stopped, upon hearing that
praise. And the Hellenes (ЕЛАНЬЕ) will become as those who
flee; and they will tell the others about the Ruthenes (РУСЬI)
-- who do not war (= kill) against them arbitrarily, but only
from a just cause. For the Greeks (ГРЬЦI) are belligerent from
their own selfishness (= desire).

____

Note in translation:

[3]Bears = BEDMEDEBA -- possibly the Witch Maidens.

____

Fyodor Izenbek's sketch of one of the original wooden
boards on which The Book of Veles had been inscribed. The
text is that of Board 17 - A. Note the two small holes in the
top-most part, for binding the individual boards together.

BREAKING NEWS!!!
Kenyan Government Releases Obama's Real Birth Certificate

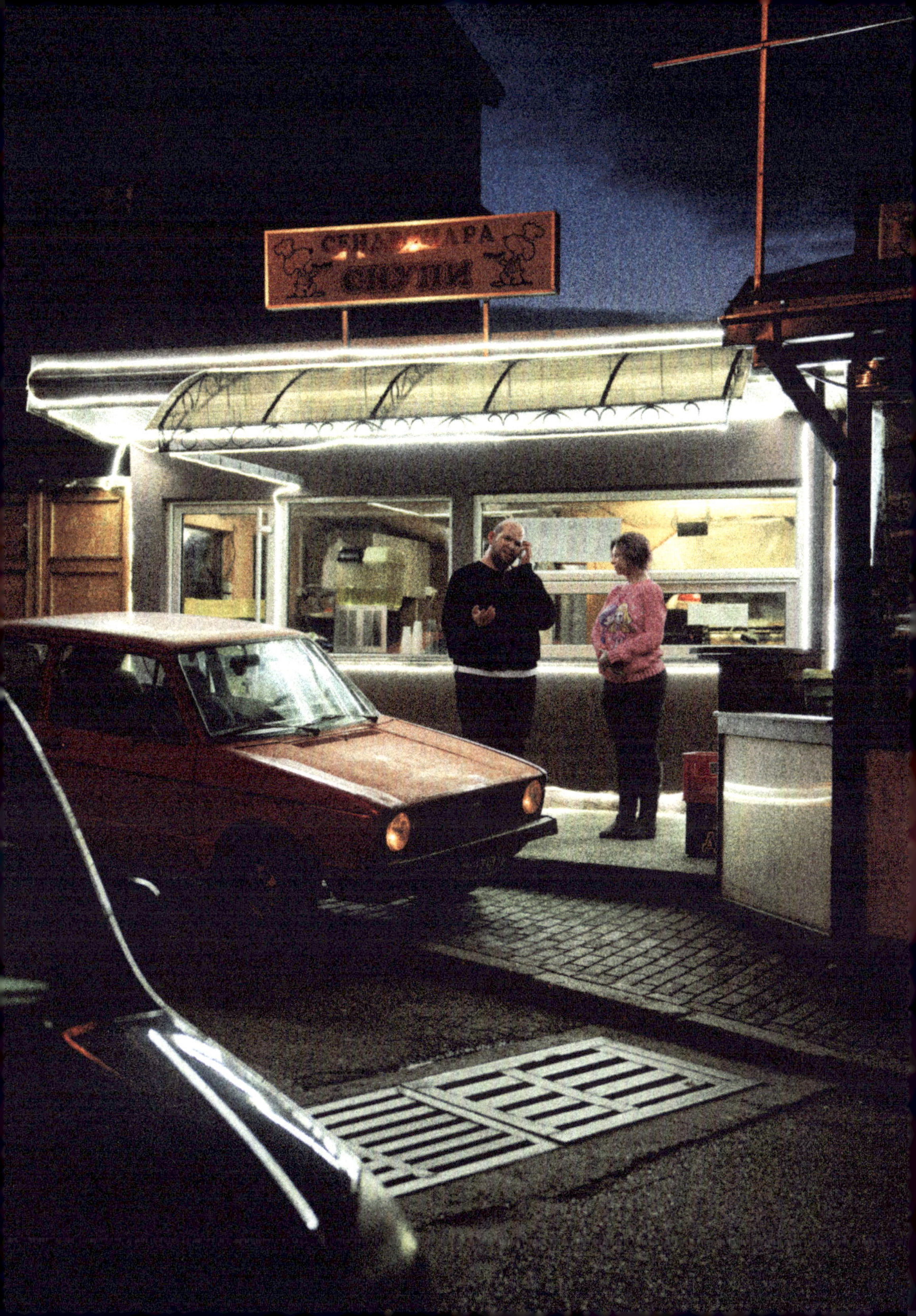

СЕНДВИЧАРА
СНУПИ

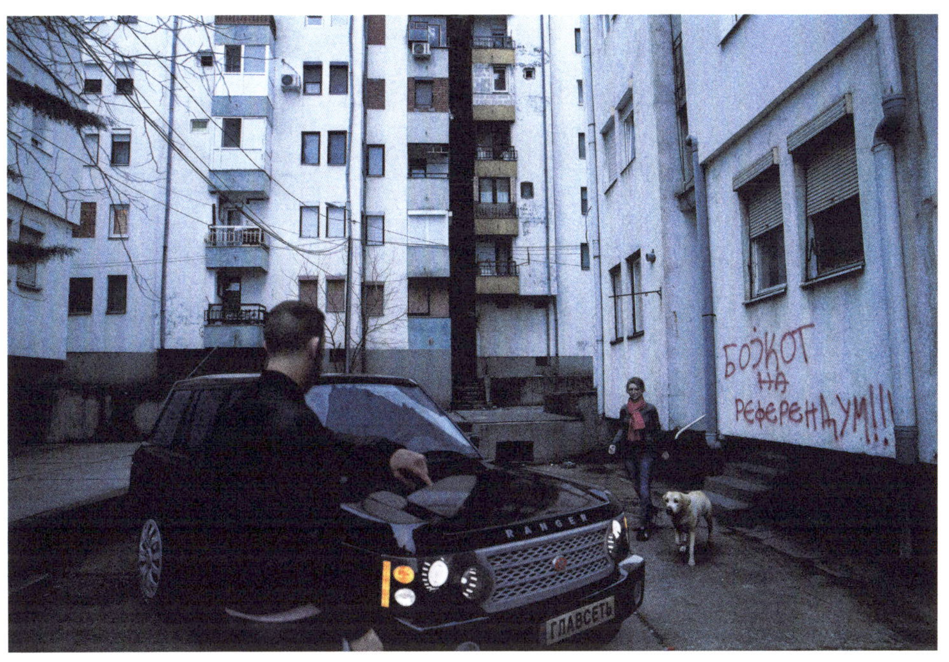

БОЈКОТ НА РЕФЕРЕНДУМ!!!
RANGER
ГЛАВСЕТЬ

"There is no moral code
in cyberspace. Cyberspace
is open to anyone with
a computer."

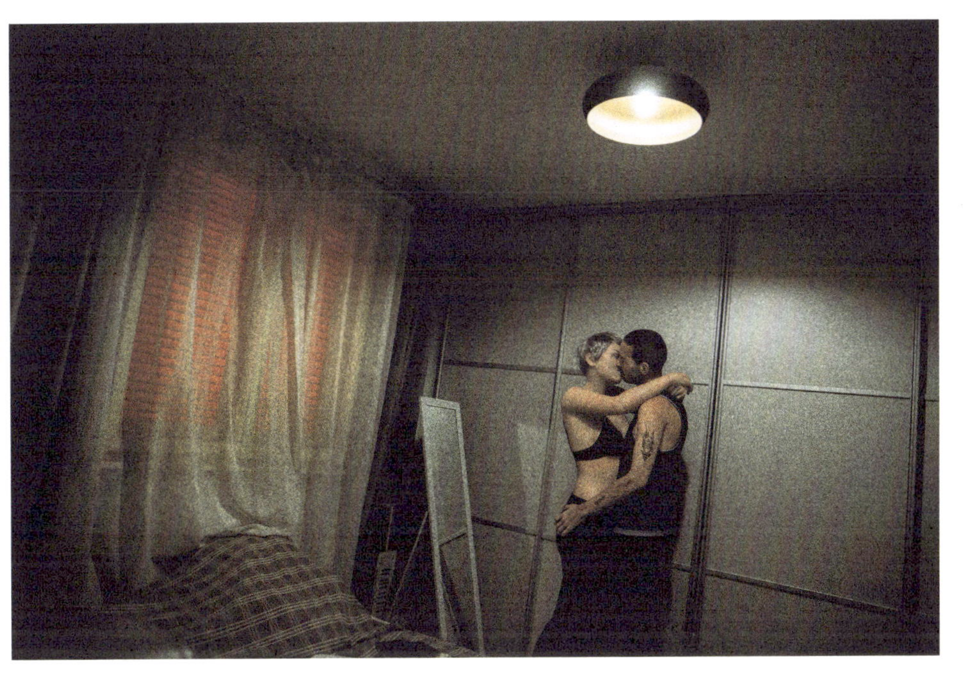

133

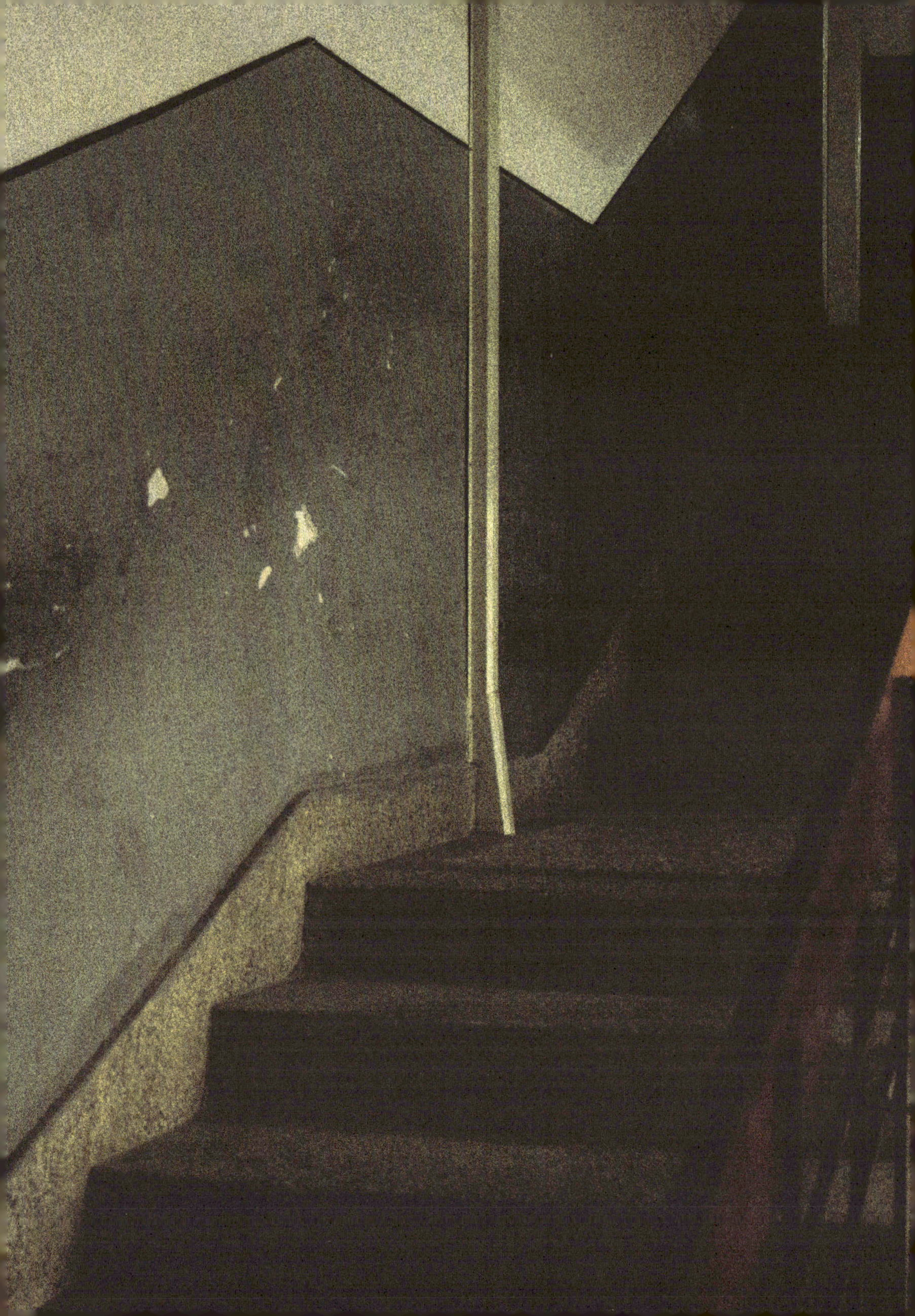

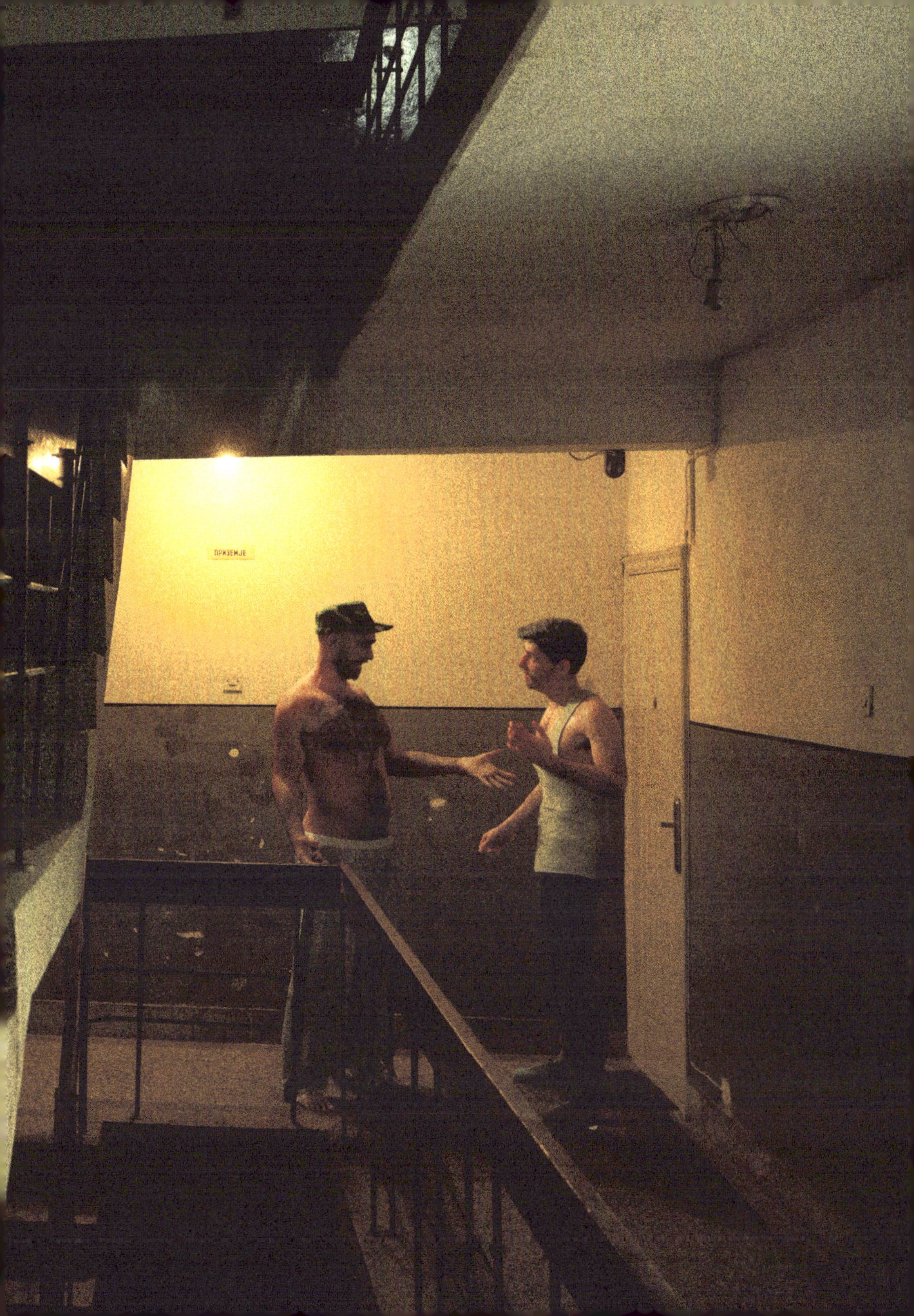

ПРИЗЕМЈЕ

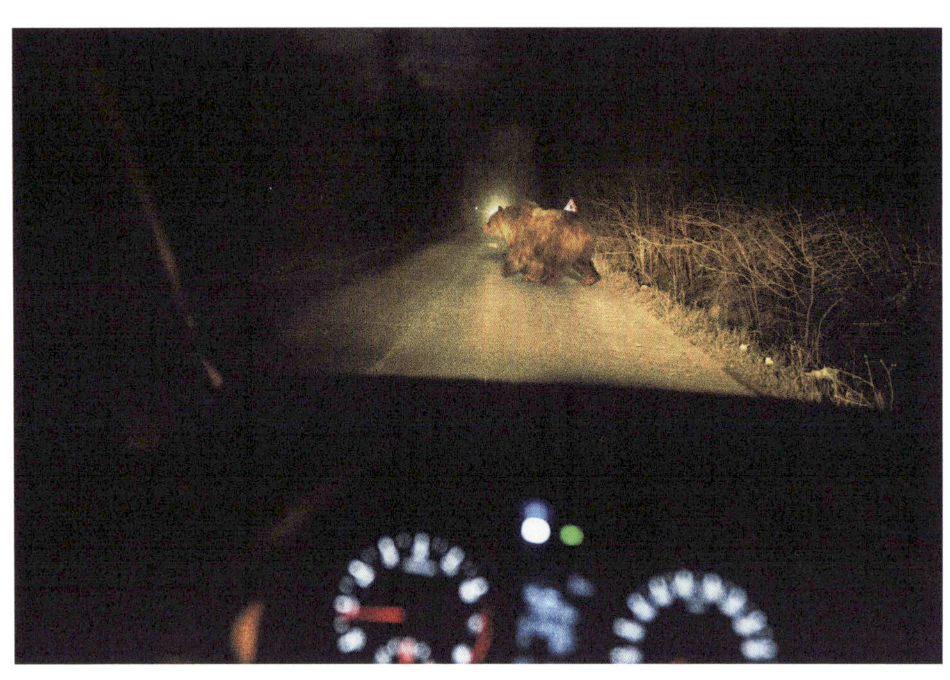

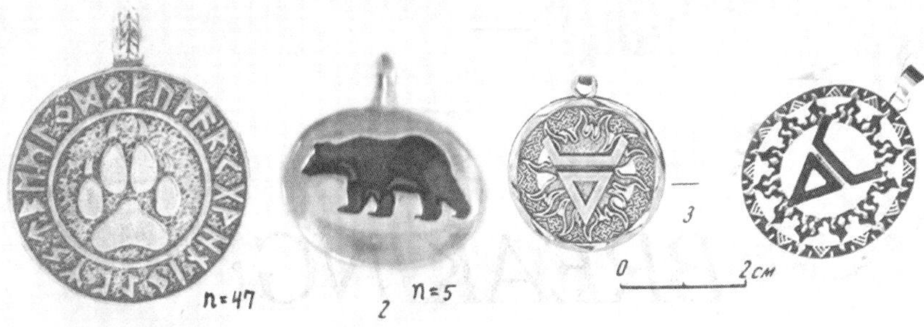

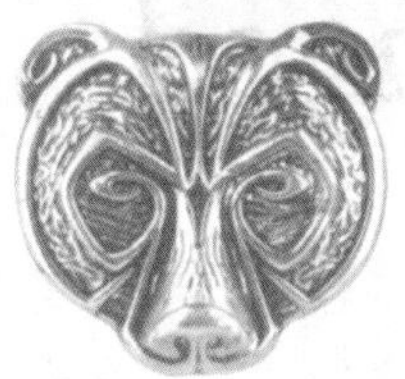

Рис. 4. Амулеты с выемчатой эмалью XI—XIII вв.

1 — из кургана 1 близ дер. Зикеево Калужской обл.;
2 — из кургана 63 близ дер. Казаричи Брянской обл.;
3 — с городища Серенск Калужской обл.; 4 — случайная находка на территории Киевской обл.

TOTAL KNOWN: 62
KNOWN SITES: 29 (n=46)

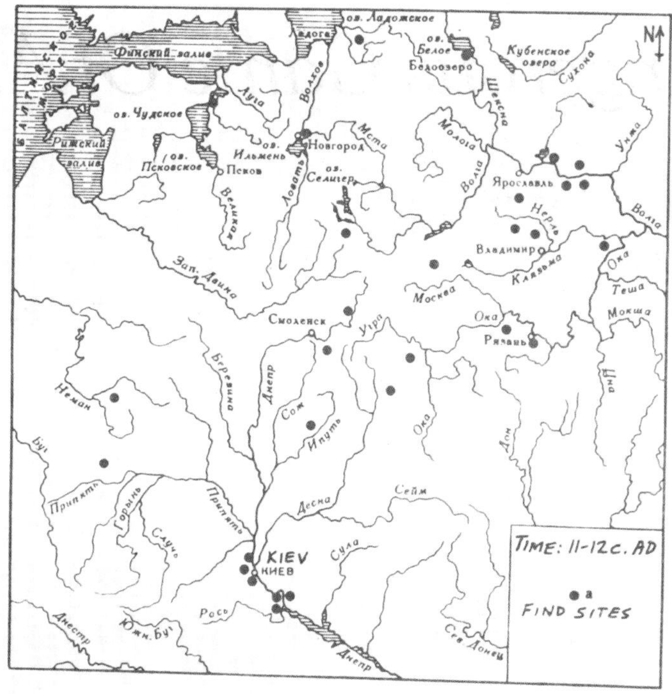

Distribution of enamel-decorated amulets in the Eastern Europe shows the spread of Veles worship. These amulets date back to the 11th-13th centuries AD.

Source: Slaviane i Rus'(in Russian), Moscow, 1968.

BREAKING:
Trump Just Challenged
Joe Biden
To The Most
Dangerous Game Of All…

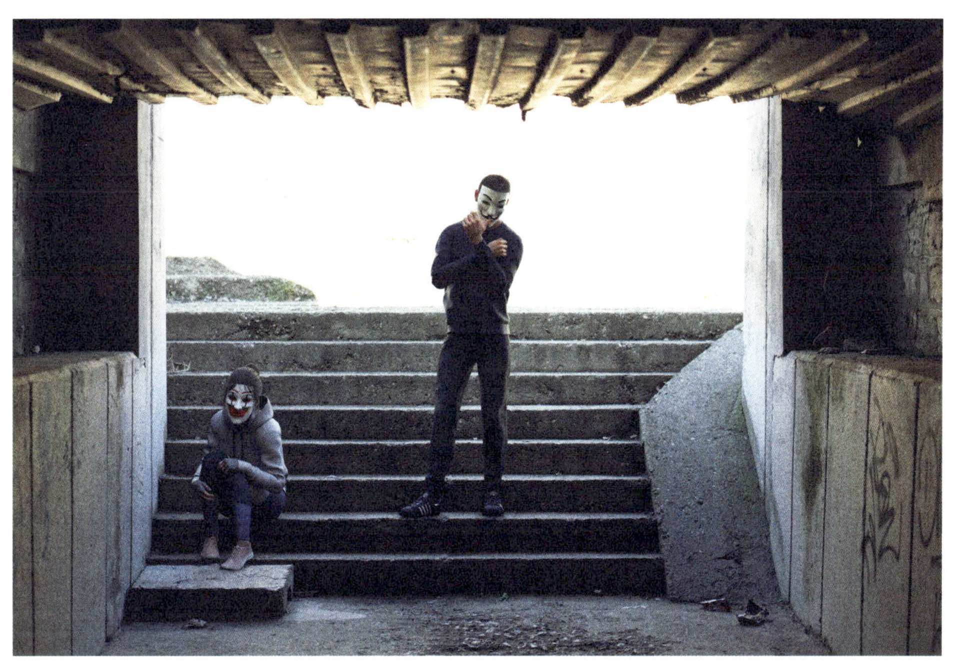

**"We didn't break
the law, we just
made a mess of it."**

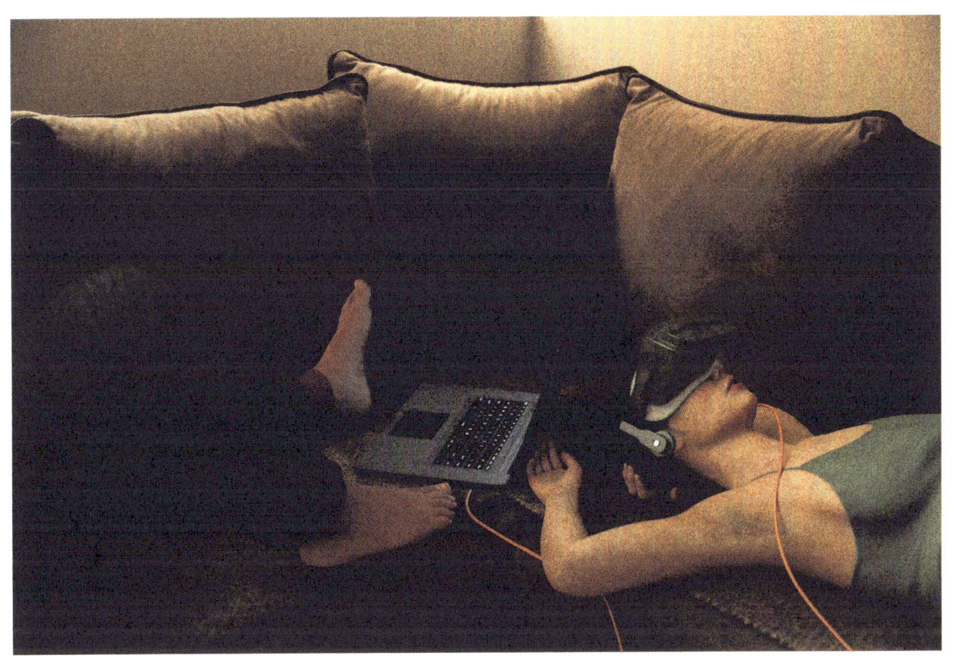

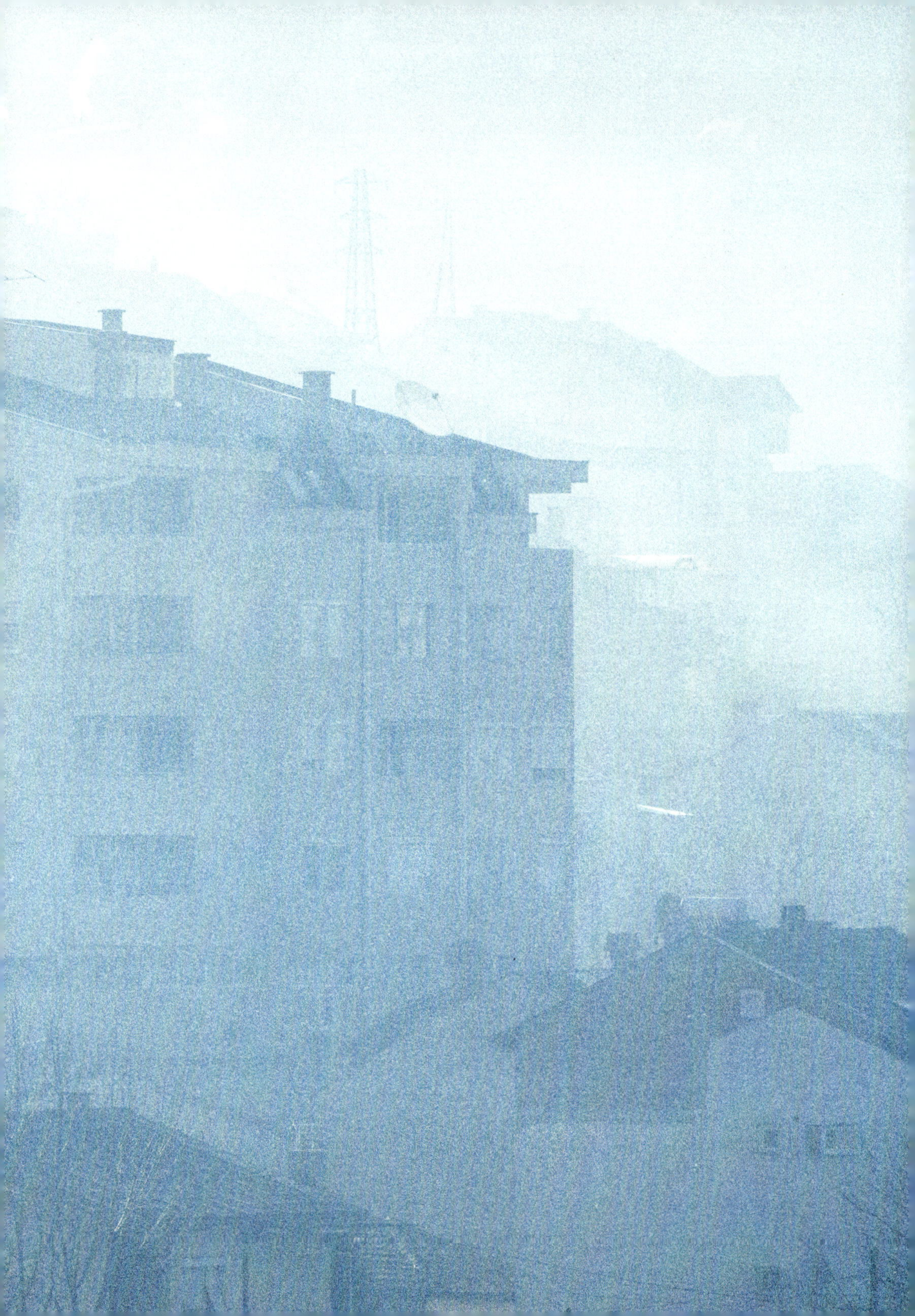

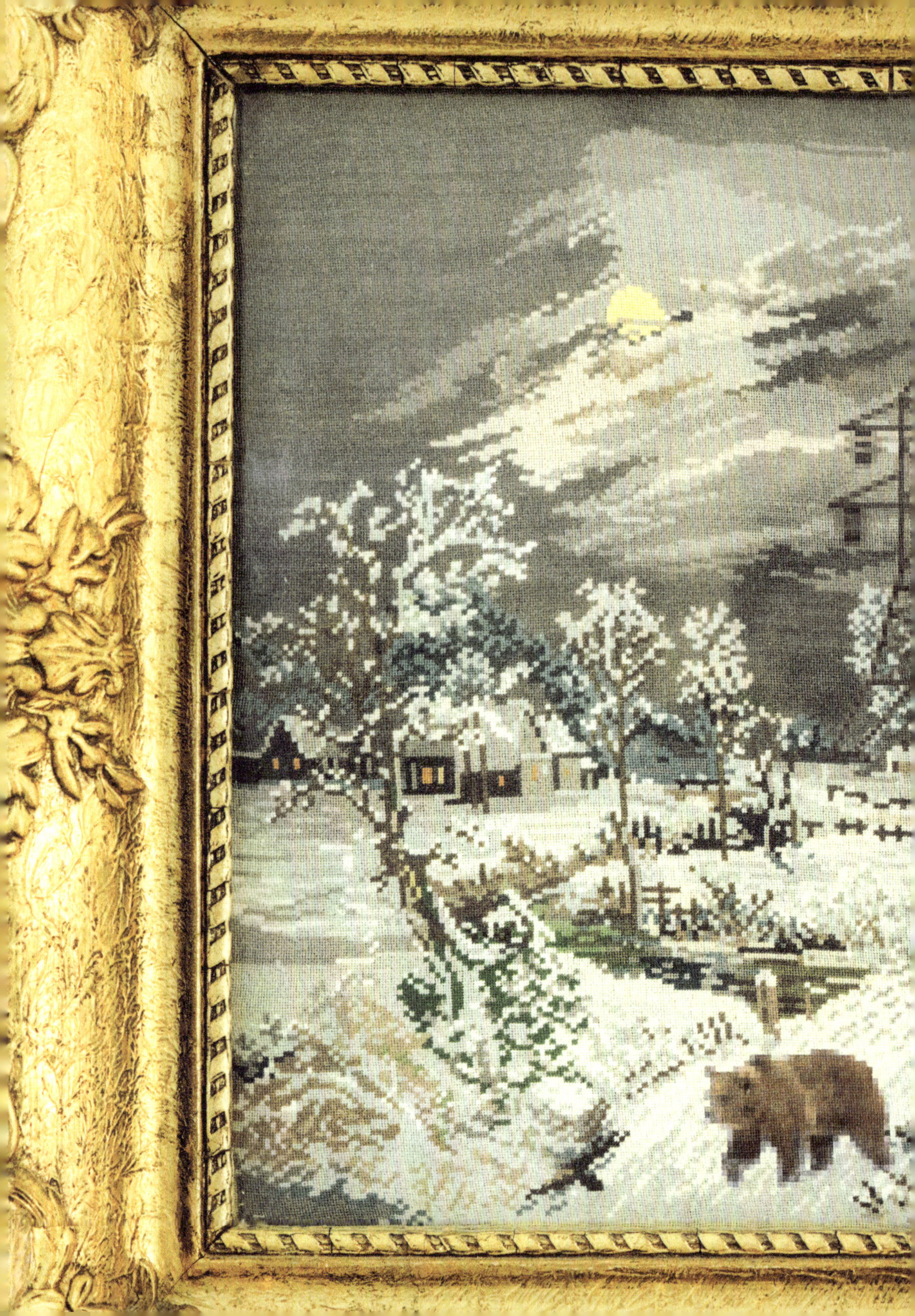

Article   Talk

Veles (god)

From Wikipedia, the free encyclopedia

This article **needs additional citations for** verification. Please help improve this article
Find sources: "Veles" god – news · newspapers · books · scholar · JSTOR *(September 2009) (Learn ho*

Veles (Cyrillic Bulgarian, Macedonian, Serbian and Ukrainian: Велес; Polish: **Weles**; Bosnian, Croatian, Czech, Montenegrin, Sl
romanized: Vialies), also known as **Volos**, or **Vles** (Russian: Волос, Влас, Власий), is a major Slavic god of earth, waters, and th
trickery, wealth, chaos and disguise. According to reconstruction by some researchers, he is the opponent of the supreme thunde
in the belief of the pagan Slavs Veles most often took the form of a bear with drooping hairy ears.[2]:141[3]:87,88 His tree is the will
speculate that he may directly continue aspects of the Proto-Indo-European pantheon.[citation needed]

Contents [hide]

1 Sources

2 Etymology

3 Enemy of Perun and storm myth

4 God of magic and musicians

5 Post-Christian Veles

6 Honors

7 See also

8 Notes

9 References

Sources   [edit]

Veles is one of few Slavic gods for which evidence of offerings can be found in all Slavic nations. The *Book of Veles*, a historical
mentioning Veles (or Vles). Here, Veles is described as a shapeshifter who operates through sorcery and deception, and who wi
White Army officer Fyodor Izenbek was inscribed on some 40 wooden boards in an proto-slavic language. After the defeat of the
library and museum. In 1925 he settled in Brussels, where he gave the planks to Yuriy Mirolyubov, who was the first to study the
unreadable) and finally translated the text. He managed to transcribe most of the planks.[citation needed]

The planks were on average 38 cm wide, 22 cm tall and about 0.5 cm thick. The surfaces of the planks were uneven, and the te
were drawn across the planks and the tops of letters were aligned with these lines. The size and shape of the letters varied, sug

In August 1941 Nazi Germany occupied Brussels, Izenbek died and the planks were lost. Mirolyubov emigrated to the United Sta
Zhar-Ptitsa (Жар-птица, "Firebird") from March 1957 until May 1959. Later the text was studied by Sergey Paramonov (Lesnoy)

Veles or Vles was one of seven gods whose statues Vladimir I of Kiev had erected in his city. Worship of Perun and Veles had to

A similar pattern can be observed among the South Slavs. Here the name of Veles appears only in toponyms, the best-known o
Herzegovina, a part of Sarajevo is called Velešići[4] and a mountain Velež[5][circular reference] near Mostar, Herzegovina.

Etymology   [edit]

Presumably it is not possible to conclusively determine a definite etymology for the name of the god Veles, though there are sev

One possibility is that the name derives from the Proto-Indo-European root *wel-, meaning wool.[6] This seems plausible, since i
World[2]:136,154 and Veles is the shepherd of the dead. *Volos* is also the Russian and Ukrainian word for "hair" and Veles is hairy

Authenticity [edit]

Most of the scholars that specialize in the field of mythological studies and Slavic linguistics (such as Boris Rybakov, Andrey Zaliznyak, Leo Klein, and all Russian academic historians and linguists) consider it a forgery.[2] According to these scholars the thorough analysis of the book shows that it was written sometime in the 20th century. The history of the book can be reliably traced only as far as mid-1950s, when the transcribed book and the photograph of one of the planks first appeared in a San Francisco-based, Russian émigré newspaper. Several scholars believe that the entire book is a product of collaboration of the editors of this newspaper and Yuriy Mirolyubov, who later claimed to have found the book. Others believe that either the entire book or the only plank available, were forged in the early 19th century by the Russian collector and forger Alexander Sulakadzev.

The book is written in a language using for the most part Slavic roots and different affixes found also in old East Slavic. Consequently, a large part of the book's text, once transcribed into a modern alphabet, is readable (albeit with some difficulty) by modern speakers of Slavic languages. However, professional linguists and historians, particularly the specialists in ancient Slavic, question many features of its language — vocabulary (modern or medieval Slavic words occasionally and unwittingly used in place of their ancient equivalents), spelling, phonetics (distinct reflections of the nasal vowels, both following Polish and Serbian patterns in different places, the haphazard handling of reduced vowels, etc., etc.), grammar (grammatical forms incompatible with early Slavic languages, combinations of affixes that contradict each other in meaning), etc. These features seem to indicate that the text was artificially "aged" by someone with superficial knowledge of ancient Slavic, and cannot be adequately translated because of lack of any consistent grammar system. In the words of the philologist O.V. Tvorogov:

> This analysis leads us to a definite conclusion: we are dealing with an artificial language, "invented" by a person unacquainted with the history of Slavic languages and one who could not create his own language system.
>
> — [3]

In Ukraine, whereas academic scholars agree that the book is a hoax, it became very popular among politicians who consider it genuine and believe it describes real historical facts relevant for establishing Ukrainian ethnicity. In particular, Levko Lukyanenko was citing the Book of Veles as historical. In 1999, the book was included in the high school program in Ukraine as a genuine literary and historical piece.[4]

To Boe. Be curious.

My deepest gratitude to Anna, Milo, Boe and Billie, for all the evenings I spent in my basement cave.

Thank you, Stuart Smith, for always being someone who gets it. And for all the cheese. Thank you to Claudia Paladini and all the other wonderful people at GOST Books.

Thanks to Julie Hrncirova and Vladimir Tevcev for the help on the ground, Mathias Gatti for the coding, Bob Demper for the library mission, and Guy Martin for inspiration and tips. Thanks to Espen Rasmussen, Frode Fjerdingstad and Håvard Bråthen for good neighbourly support, and to Lars Wabø for the drone piloting.

This work would not have been possible without the financial support from the Freedom of Expression Foundation, the Arts Council Norway, the Norwegian Photographic Fund, and Boston Consulting Group. Thank you to Bente Roalsvig and Massimo Portincaso.

A big thank you to everyone at Magnum Photos. Special thanks to Olivia Arthur, Caitlin Hughes, Thomas Dworzak, Christopher Anderson, Peter van Agtmael, Sophie Wright, Michael Sargeant and Shannon Ghannam.

Thanks to OpenAI, Daz, Blender and NVIDIA. What fun toys.

Last, but certainly not least; a nice big bear hug to Chloe Miskin.

Third printing 2022
First published in 2021 by
GOST Books, London

info@gostbooks.com
gostbooks.com

The Book of Veles
© GOST Books
Images and text © Jonas Bendiksen

Pages 5, 8-16, 41, 51, 61, 81, 101, 111, 131, 141 and 151 are based on the 1973 translation of *The Book of Vles (Vles Knyha)* © Victor Kachur

Edited and designed by GOST:
Rossella Castello, Katie Clifford, Gemma Gerhard, Justine Hucker, Allon Kaye, Eleanor Macnair, Claudia Paladini, Ana Rocha

Printed in Italy by EBS

British Library cataloguing-in-publication data. A catalogue record of this book is available from the British Library.

ISBN 978-1-910401-61-3

Январь
Февраль
Март
Декабрь
Соухвiй
Апрель
Просинецъ Сѣченъ
Ноябрь
Берёзозоl
Грудень
Студены
Берестъ
Травень
Май
Октябрь
Листопадъ Паздерник
Кресень Изокъ
Сентябрь
Рюень
Июнь
Серпень Зарева
Червень
Август
Июль

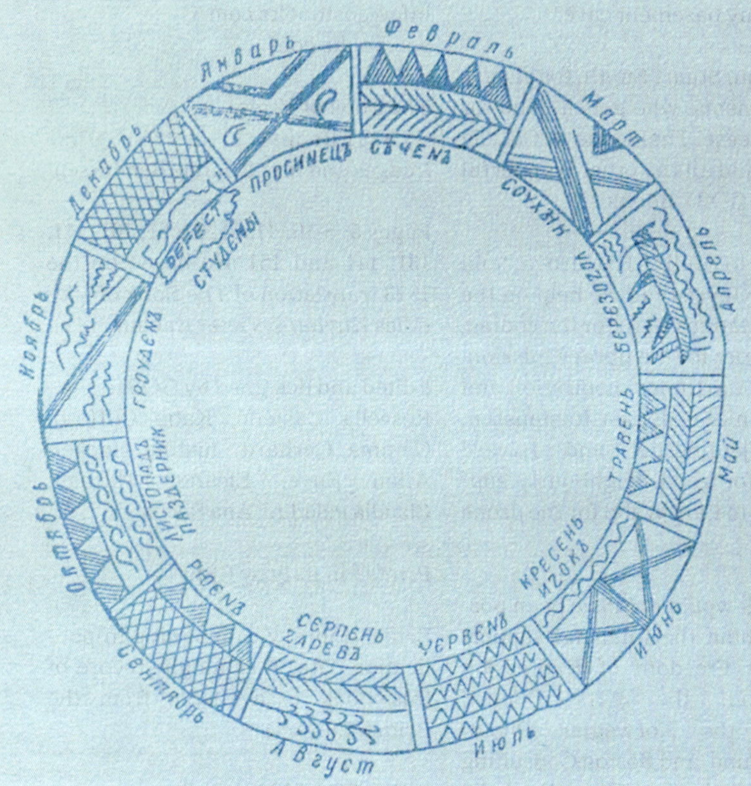

THE END

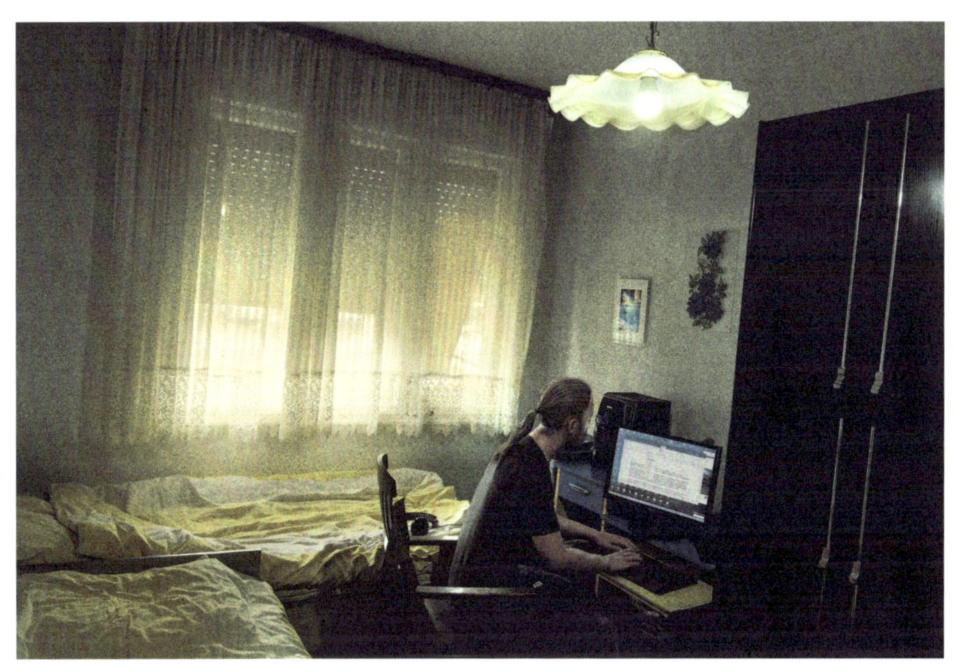

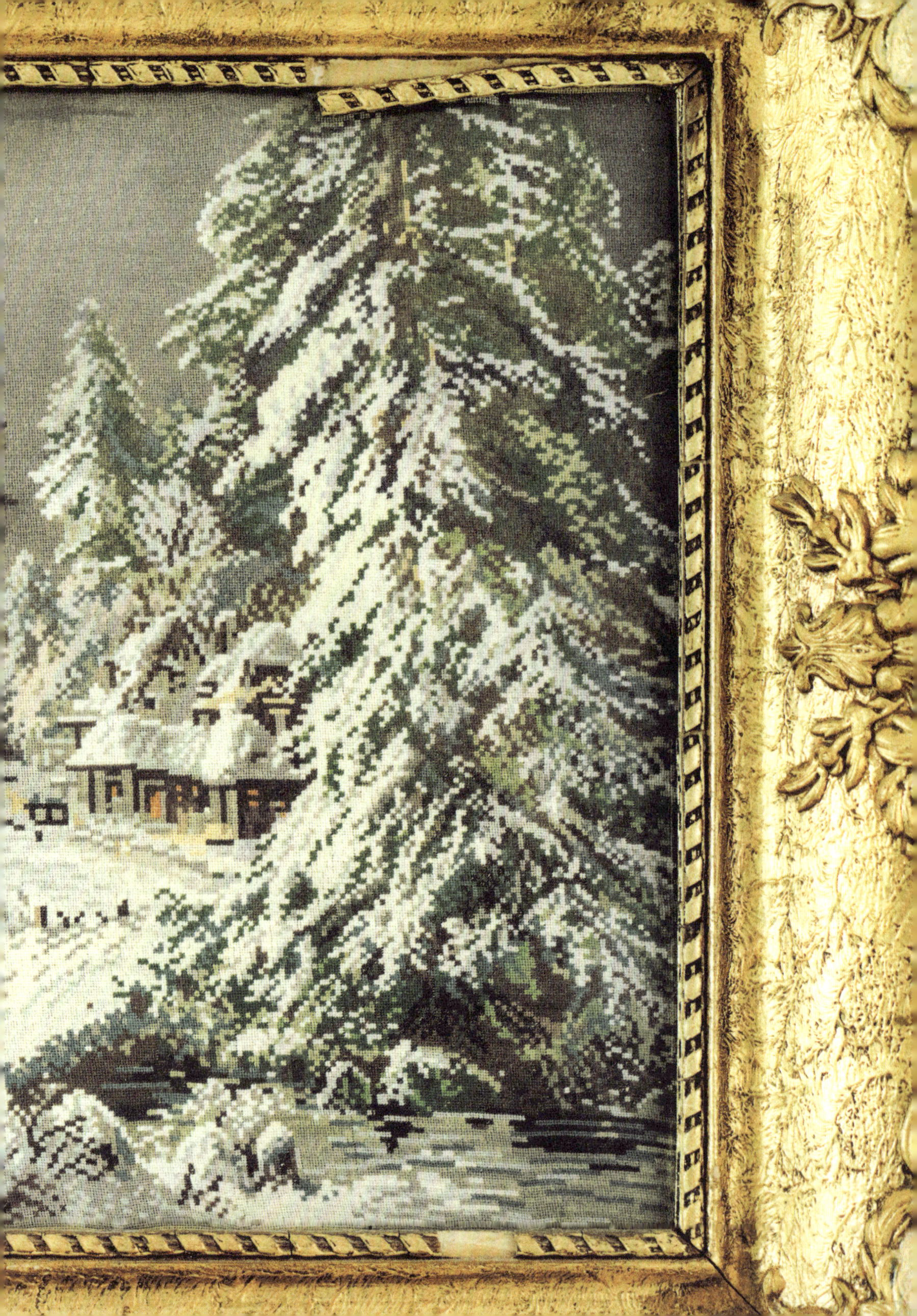